BIBLICAL HEBREW

A COMPACT GUIDE

Other Resources by Miles V. Van Pelt

English Grammar to Ace Biblical Hebrew

Basics of Biblical Hebrew Video Lectures

Basics of Biblical Hebrew Vocabulary Audio

Basics of Biblical Aramaic: Complete Grammar, Lexicon, and Annotated Text

Basics of Biblical Aramaic Video Lectures

Other Resources by Miles V. Van Pelt and Gary. D Pratico

Basics of Biblical Hebrew Grammar

Basics of Biblical Hebrew Workbook

Charts of Biblical Hebrew

Graded Reader of Biblical Hebrew

Old Testament Hebrew Vocabulary Cards

The Vocabulary Guide to Biblical Hebrew and Aramaic

Biblical Hebrew Vocabulary in Context

Biblical Hebrew Laminated Sheet

BIBLICAL HEBREW

A COMPACT GUIDE

Second Edition

MILES V. VAN PELT

ZONDERVAN ACADEMIC

ZONDERVAN ACADEMIC

Biblical Hebrew: A Compact Guide

ISBN 978-0-310-09378-7 (softcover)

Requests for information should be addressed to:
Zondervan, *3900 Sparks Dr. SE, Grand Rapids, Michigan 49546*

Cover design: LUCAS Art & Design
Typesetting: Miles V. Van Pelt

Printed in the United States of America

21 22 23 24 25 26 27 28 /CHM/ 14 13 12 11 10 9 8 7 6 5 4 3

TABLE OF CONTENTS

Nominal System

Appendices

PREFACE TO THE SECOND EDITION

This second edition of the *Compact Guide* has been updated and revised in accordance with the third edition of *Basics of Biblical Hebrew Grammar* by Gary D. Pratico and Miles V. Van Pelt (Grand Rapids: Zondervan, 2019). In addition to minor advances in typography, there is an alternative presentation of Hebrew Vowel Rules (pp. 12–13), a section on Hebrew Verbless Clauses (pp. 75–76), and an expanded lexicon that now includes all words (excluding proper names) that occur ten or more times in the Hebrew Bible.

The response to the first edition of the *Compact Guide* has been altogether encouraging. This resource has been used with profit as a means of review and as a supplement to other introductory resources. Its design is particularly helpful for use with the *Graded Reader of Biblical Hebrew* (Grand Rapids: Zondervan, 2006) and *Biblical Hebrew Vocabulary in Context* (Grand Rapids: Zondervan, 2019). It is also well suited for exegesis courses that work with the original languages.

I am indebted to the wonderful team of co-laborers at Zondervan, especially my editor and friend, Nancy Erickson. I am also grateful to Reformed Theological Seminary for providing the context from which this work emerges, and for those students who labor to study the Bible in Hebrew in order to faithfully proclaim the gospel from it. And then there is my family, who continue to show excitement and enthusiasm with my ongoing obsession to produce student-friendly language resources. You guys are the best ever!

PREFACE TO THE FIRST EDITION

This little book was written in order to provide students with a "compact guide" to biblical Hebrew. Beginning students will find the presentation of material convenient for review. Intermediate students can use this mini-grammar as a practical tool for translation. Even the veterans of this biblical language will find the compact guide helpful for blowing off the dust, filling in the cracks, and keeping fit in biblical Hebrew.

The utility of a compact guide is offset by limitations related to page length and size. The selection of content will not satisfy everyone's preferences, but we did take careful aim. The best way to access the book's content is through the extended table of contents. The material presented in this book is derived primarily from *Basics of Biblical Hebrew*, 2nd edition, by Gary D. Pratico and Miles V. Van Pelt (Zondervan, 2007).

Thanks again to my friend and editor, Verlyn Verbrugge, for all of his expert help with the production of this guide. My teaching assistants, Kelley Baldridge and Josh Drake, make it possible for me to write in the midst of a full schedule. Thanks to Paul Sumner for his careful proofreading. Finally, I am indebted to a special team of Hebrew language consultants who provided expert proofreading and content checking: Jane E. Baynard, William Baynard, Chapel Baynard, Leigh Ann King, William King, May Hudson King, and Charlie King. You guys saved my bacon!

HEBREW ALPHABET

Letter	Final Form	Name	Pronunciation
א		Alef	(silent)
ב		Bet	b as in boy
ג		Gimel	g as in God
ד		Dalet	d as in day
ה		He	h as in hay
ו		Waw	w as in way
ז		Zayin	z as in Zion
ח		Ḥet	ch as in Bach
ט		Tet	t as in toy
י		Yod	y as in yes
כ	ך	Kaf	k as in king
ל		Lamed	l as in lion
מ	ם	Mem	m as in mother
נ	ן	Nun	n as in now
ס		Samek	s as in sin
ע		Ayin	(silent)
פ	ף	Pe	p as in pastor
צ	ץ	Tsade	ts as in boots
ק		Qof	k as in king
ר		Resh	r as in run
שׂ		Sin	s as in sin
שׁ		Shin	sh as in ship
ת		Taw	t as in toy

1. **Direction**. Hebrew is written from *right to left,* not left to right as in English.

אבגדהוזחטיכלמנסעפצקרשׂשׁת

2. **Begadkephat Letters**. Six Hebrew consonants have two possible pronunciations. The presence or absence of the Daghesh Lene distinguishes between the hard or soft pronunciation of the consonant.

בּ	b as in boy	כּ	k as in king
ב	v as in vine	כ	ch as in Bach
גּ	g as in God	פּ	p as in pastor
ג	g as in aghast	פ	ph as in alphabet
דּ	d as in day	תּ	t as in toy
ד	dh as in the	ת	th as in thin

3. **Gutturals**. The guttural consonants are א, ה, ח, ע and sometimes ר behaves similarly. Gutturals (1) cannot take Daghesh Forte, (2) take Hateph vowels instead of Vocal Shewa, and (3) prefer to appear with a-class vowels. The semi-guttural ר may take Vocal Shewa.

4. **Modern Pronunciation**. Israeli Hebrew differs in a number of ways from what is considered to be the traditional or ancient pronunciation.

Consonant	Traditional Pronunciation	Modern Pronunciation
ג	g as in giant	g as in God
ד	dh as in the	d as in day
ת	th as in thin	t as in toy
ו	w as in way	v as in vine

HEBREW VOWELS

Hebrew vowels can be divided into two groups: regular vowels and vowel letters. In each group, there are as many as five vowel classes (a, e, i, o, u). The regular vowels are presented in three major categories: long, short, and reduced. The vowel letters are organized by the consonant with which they appear (He, Waw, and Yod).

Regular Vowels

Long Vowels

a-class	בָ	Qamets	a as in father
e-class	בֵ	Tsere	e as in they
o-class	בֹ	Holem	o as in role

Short Vowels

a-class	בַ	Pathach	a as in bat
e-class	בֶ	Seghol	e as in better
i-class	בִ	Hireq	i as in bitter
o-class	בָ	Qamets Hatuf	o as in bottle
u-class	בֻ	Qibbuts	u as in ruler

Reduced (Hateph) Vowels

a-class	בֲ	Hateph Pathach	a as in amuse
e-class	בֱ	Hateph Seghol	e as in metallic
o-class	בֳ	Hateph Qamets	o as in commit

Vowel Letters

Vowel Letters Written with ה (He)

a-class	בָה	Qamets He	a as in father
e-class	בֵה	Tsere He	e as in they
	בֶה	Seghol He	e as in better
o-class	בֹה	Holem He	o as in role

Vowel Letters Written with ו (Waw)

o-class	בוֹ	Holem Waw	o as in role
u-class	בוּ	Shureq	u as in ruler

Vowel Letters Written with י (Yod)

e-class	בֵי	Tsere Yod	e as in they
	בֶי	Seghol Yod	e as in better
i-class	בִי	Hireq Yod	i as in machine

Notes on Hebrew Vowel Letters

1. Vowel letters written with ה (He) occur only at the end of a word, as in תּוֹרָה (law) and יִבְנֶה (he will build).
2. Vowel letters written with ו (Waw) and י (Yod) are often referred to as unchangeable or historically long vowels.
3. Defective writing is that phenomenon in which certain vowel letters are written without their consonant. There are three patterns of defective writing.

בוֹ ➢ בֹ Holem Waw written as Holem

בוּ ➢ בֻ Shureq written as Qibbuts

בִי ➢ בִ Hireq Yod written as Hireq

Other Symbols

1. **Daghesh Lene** (בּ) appears as a small dot only in a *begadkephat* consonant in order to distinguish between the hard and soft pronunciations.
2. **Daghesh Forte** (בּ) doubles the consonant in which it appears. It can occur in any consonant except the gutturals and ר.
3. **Mappiq** (הּ) identifies ה as a consonant and not a vowel letter. It appears only in ה at the end of a word and should not be confused with the Daghesh Lene or the Daghesh Forte.
4. **Silent Shewa** (בְ) has a zero value and is never pronounced and never transliterated.
5. **Vocal Shewa** (בְ) maintains a hurried pronunciation and sounds like the *a* in amuse.

SYLLABIFICATION

Two Rules of Syllabification

1. Every syllable must begin with one consonant and have only one vowel.[1] For example, the word דָּבָר is syllabified as דָּ|בָר. This example has two syllables, each beginning with a consonant and each having only one vowel.

2. There are only two types of syllables: open and closed. Open syllables end with a vowel and closed syllables end with a consonant. With the word דָּבָר, the syllable דָּ is open because it ends with a vowel (Qamets) and the syllable בָר is closed because it ends with a consonant (ר).

Syllable Classification

1. **Tonic**. The accented syllable is called the tonic syllable. In the example דָּבָר, the final syllable בָר is the tonic syllable because it is the accented syllable. In the example סֵ֫פֶר, the first syllable סֵ֫ is the tonic syllable because it is the accented syllable.

2. **Pretonic**. Syllables in the pretonic position occur *before* the tonic syllable. In the example דָּבָר, the syllable דָּ is pretonic because it occurs *before* the tonic syllable.

---

1. There is only one exception to this rule. It occurs with the spelling of the conjunction וְ as וּ (Shureq).

3. **Post-tonic**. Syllables in the post-tonic position occur *after* the tonic syllable. In the example סֵ֫פֶר, the syllable פֶר is post-tonic because it occurs *after* the tonic syllable.

4. **Propretonic**. Syllables occurring *before the pretonic syllable* are called propretonic syllables. In the examples דְּבָרִים (syllabified as דְּ|בָ|רִים) and סְפָרִים (syllabified as סְ|פָ|רִים), the syllables דְּ and סְ are propretonic syllables because they occur *before the pretonic syllable*. Note that a Hebrew word can have only one tonic, pretonic, or post-tonic syllable. However, there may be multiple propretonic syllables in a Hebrew word.

5. An alternative system of syllable classification also exists for which the location of the accent is not determinative. In this system, the *ultima* is the last syllable of a word. The *penultima* is the next-to-last syllable, and the *antepenultima* is the syllable before the penultima.

6. In addition to the "tonic" and "ultima" systems of syllable classification, it is not uncommon for syllables to be referred to simply as *accented* or *unaccented*, especially with reference to closed syllables.

The Daghesh and Syllabification

1. The **Daghesh Lene** *does not* impact syllabification. It simply indicates the hard sound of the *begadkephat* letter in which it appears.

2. The **Daghesh Forte** *does* impact syllabification because it doubles the value of the consonant in which it appears. For example, the Hebrew word חֻקָּה is syllabified as חֻקְ|קָה, rendering the ק two times because of the presence of the Daghesh Forte.

3. The Daghesh in a *begadkephat* letter may be either Daghesh Forte or Daghesh Lene. If the Daghesh is immediately preceded by a vowel, it is Daghesh Forte. For example, the Daghesh in אַתָּה is Daghesh Forte because it is immediately preceded by a vowel (Pathach).

4. If the Daghesh is *not* immediately preceded by a vowel, it is Daghesh Lene. For example, the Daghesh in מַלְכָּה is Daghesh Lene because it is *not* immediately preceded by a vowel (it is preceded by ל with Silent Shewa).

5. A *begadkephat* letter at the beginning of a word takes a Daghesh Lene unless the previous word ends in a vowel (e.g., בָּרַךְ, גּוֹי, or דָּבָר).

The Shewa and Syllabification

1. The Shewa always marks the termination of a syllable. The **Silent Shewa** marks the end of a closed syllable and the **Vocal Shewa** marks the end of an open syllable. Thus, you can always divide a syllable after Shewa.

2. The Shewa is *silent* if the preceding vowel is short. For example, the Shewa in מַלְכָּה must be *silent* because it is immediately preceded by the short vowel Pathach.

3. The Shewa is *vocal* if not immediately preceded by a short vowel. For example, the Shewas in בְּרָכָה and כֹּתְבִים must be *vocal* because they are not immediately preceded by a short vowel.[2]

4. A Shewa under a consonant with Daghesh Forte is doubled with the consonant, the first being silent and the second being vocal. For example, the noun הַמְּלָכִים is syllabified as הַמְ|מְ|לָ|כִים. Observe how מְּ is rendered מְ|מְ in syllabification. In the first instance, the Shewa is silent, terminating a closed syllable הַמְ. In the next instance, the Shewa is vocal, terminating an open syllable מְ.

Rules of Shewa

1. **The First Rule of Shewa**. Hebrew will not allow two contiguous (side-by-side) Vocal Shewas at the beginning of a word. In such a circumstance, the first Vocal Shewa becomes Hireq and the second Vocal Shewa becomes Silent Shewa. In other words, two Vocal Shewas become a single syllable in which there are no Vocal Shewas. For example, the prefixing of the preposition לְ (to, for) to נְבִיאִים (prophets) would produce לְנְבִיאִים but two Vocal Shewas are not allowed at the beginning of a word. The application of the first Rule of Shewa produces לִנְבִיאִים (Hireq in a closed syllable).

---

2. Gutturals will not appear with a Vocal Shewa but rather take one of the Hateph vowels. Consonants with a Hateph vowel are always considered open and unaccented.

2. **Exception to the First Rule of Shewa**. The application of the first Rule of Shewa produces a different spelling if the word begins with the syllable יְ as in יְהוּדָה (Judah). The prefixing of the preposition לְ (to) to יְהוּדָה would produce לְיְהוּדָה, but two Vocal Shewas at the beginning of a word are not allowed. In this case, the application of the Rule of Shewa produces לִיהוּדָה (to Judah) with Hireq Yod.

3. **The Second Rule of Shewa**. A second Rule of Shewa applies to syllables that have a guttural consonant followed by a Hateph vowel. For example, the prefixing of the preposition בְּ (in) to חֲלוֹם (dream) would produce בְּחֲלוֹם but this combination of syllables is not allowed. A Vocal Shewa cannot precede a guttural with a Hateph vowel. Application of the second Rule of Shewa produces בַּחֲלוֹם (in a dream). With this spelling, the preposition takes *the corresponding short vowel* (Pathach) *of the reduced vowel* (Hateph Pathach).

4. **Exception to the Second Rule of Shewa**. There is one important exception to the second Rule of Shewa. When an inseparable preposition like לְ is prefixed to אֱלֹהִים (God), the result is לֵאלֹהִים (to God). This spelling is occasioned by the א becoming quiescent and then compensatory lengthening (Seghol lengthens to Tsere).

Qamets and Qamets Hatuf

1. The Qamets indicates the long a-class vowel and the Qamets Hatuf indicates the short o-class vowel. However, their forms (בָּ) are identical.

2. The **Qamets Hatuf** occurs only in closed, unaccented syllables, as in חָכְמָה or כָּל־. The Qamets never appears in a closed, unaccented syllable.

3. The **Qamets** occurs in open, pretonic syllables or in closed accented syllables. In the example דָּבָר, the Qamets vowel appears in both syllables.

4. In certain ambiguous situations, Hebrew employs the **Metheg** (a small vertical stroke to the left of the vowel), to identify the Qamets (long a-class) vowel, as in בָּֽתִּים, syllabified as בָּֽ|תִּים.

Additional Issues for Syllabification

1. **Furtive Pathach**. When a word ends with ח or ע (not immediately preceded by an a-class vowel), a Pathach may appear beneath this final guttural consonant, as in רוּחַ or רָקִיעַ. This use of the Pathach is called the Furtive Pathach and it is pronounced *before* the final guttural consonant. In terms of syllabification, the Furtive Pathach is not counted (e.g. רָ|קִיעַ).

2. **Quiescent א**. When א occurs in a word without a vowel, it is quiescent, as in חַטָּאת (sin). When the א is quiescent, it is not considered to be a consonant with reference to the rules of syllabification. (e.g., חַטְ|טָאת).

3. **Hebrew Diphthongs**. Diphthong is a grammatical term used to identify sounds normally distinct, but now functioning as a single unit. The most common Hebrew diphthong is the AY diphthong, consisting of the accented unit Pathach-Yod-Hireq, as in שָׁמַ֫יִם or בַּ֫יִת. There is also the AW diphthong, consisting of the accented unit Qamets-Waw-Seghol, as in מָ֫וֶת or אָ֫וֶן. Syllables that contain a diphthong are considered (as a unit) to be closed because they end with a consonant (e.g., שָׁ|מַ֫יִם).

Hebrew Vowel Rules. A vowel's preference for a particular type of syllable is determined by two primary factors: (1) the type of syllable (open or closed) and (2) the proximity of the syllable to the accent (accented/unaccented, or tonic/pretonic/propretonic).[3]

Closed Syllables. Closed syllables are classified as either accented or unaccented.

1. In a **closed accented** syllable, Hebrew prefers a long vowel (דָּ|בָר).
2. In a **closed unaccented** Syllable, Hebrew requires a short vowel (מֶ֫|לֶךְ).

Open Syllables. Open syllables are classified as either tonic, pretonic (post-tonic), or propretonic.

---

3. The following rules are derived and adapted from Russell T. Fuller and Kyoungwon Choi, *Invitation to Biblical Hebrew: A Beginning Grammar* (Grand Rapids: Kregel Publications, 2006), 25–26.

1. In an **open tonic** syllable, Hebrew prefers a short vowel (מֶ֫|לֶךְ).
2. In an **open pretonic** (and post-tonic) syllable, Hebrew requires a long vowel (דָּ|בָר).
3. In an originally **open propretonic** syllable, Hebrew requires Vocal Shewa or a Hateph vowel with guttural consonants (דְּ|בָ|רִים or אֱ|לֹ|הִים).

Additional Vowel Characteristics

1. Vowel letters written with Waw or Yod do not reduce to shorter vowels, though they may be written defectively. For this reason, they are often called "unchangeable" long vowels. Other grammars may list them as "historically" long vowels.
2. Guttural consonants: (a) cannot take Daghesh Forte; (b) take Hateph vowels instead of Vocal Shewa; and (c) prefer a-class vowels.
3. The rejection of the Daghesh Forte by Gutturals can cause compensatory lengthening, virtual doubling, or the appearance of an irregular Seghol vowel.
4. *Sqnmlwy*. This mnemonic identifies all "s" type consonants in Hebrew (ס, צ, שׂ, and שׁ), plus the letters q (ק), n (נ), m (מ), l (ל), w (ו), and y (י) – thus, *sqnmlwy*! When one of these letters appears with a Daghesh Forte *and* a Vocal Shewa, the Daghesh Forte will frequently drop out (e.g., הַמְּרַגְּלִים becomes הַמְרַגְּלִים or וַיְּהִי becomes וַיְהִי). This is the *sqnmlwy* phenomenon.

NOUNS

Noun Paradigm

In terms of gender, Hebrew nouns are either masculine *or* feminine (though a few are both masculine *and* feminine). In terms of number, Hebrew nouns may be singular, plural, or dual (meaning "two"). A noun's gender and number can be identified by the type of ending that appears on the noun.

	Masculine		Feminine	
Singular	סוּס	horse	תּוֹרָה	law
Plural	סוּסִים	horses	תּוֹרוֹת	laws
Dual	סוּסַ֫יִם	two horses	תּוֹרָתַ֫יִם	two laws

Noun Paradigm Notes

1. The lexical (dictionary) form for any noun is the singular form.

2. Masculine nouns are endingless, but some feminine nouns are endingless too, as in אֶ֫רֶץ (land), יָד (hand), and עִיר (city).

3. Most feminine singular nouns end with Qamets He, as in שָׁנָה (year), אִשָּׁה (woman), and מִלְחָמָה (war). Some feminine singular nouns end with Taw, as in בַּת (daughter), חַטָּאת (sin), and בְּרִית (covenant).

4. The feminine plural ending וֹת is sometimes spelled with Holem instead of Holem Waw. For example, the feminine plural form תּוֹרוֹת (full or *plene* spelling) may be spelled as תּוֹרֹת (short or defective spelling). With the short form, there is no change in pronunciation or translation.

Noun Pluralization and Vocalization

When a noun is pluralized, the accent and syllable structure of the noun may change. Changes of this type will frequently impact the vocalization (vowels) of the pluralized noun. Knowing the types of changes that can occur is essential for identification and translation.

1. **No Change**. Some nouns will pluralize without any change in vocalization. These nouns include: (a) monosyllabic nouns with an unchangeable long vowel, as in שִׁיר; and (b) two-syllable nouns with Vocal Shewa (or a Hateph vowel) in the first syllable and an unchangeable long vowel in the second syllable, as in חֲלוֹם.

שִׁיר	song	➢	שִׁירִים	songs
אוֹת	sign	➢	אוֹתוֹת	signs
חֲלוֹם	dream	➢	חֲלוֹמוֹת	dreams
רְחוֹב	street	➢	רְחוֹבוֹת	streets

2. **Propretonic Reduction**. Two syllable nouns accented on the second syllable with a long vowel in the first syllable will undergo propretonic reduction in that first syllable. In other words, the long vowel in the first syllable will reduce to Vocal Shewa (or a Hateph vowel).

דָּבָר	word	➢	דְּבָרִים	words
לֵבָב	heart	➢	לְבָבוֹת	hearts
עָנָן	cloud	➢	עֲנָנִים	clouds
חָצֵר	courtyard	➢	חֲצֵרוֹת	courtyards

3. **Segholate Nouns**. Two-syllable nouns accented on the first syllable, as in מֶ֫לֶךְ or בַּ֫עַל, are called Segholate nouns. In the singular, the vowel pattern of a Segholate noun may vary (as the two examples above demonstrate). In the plural, however, all Segholate nouns follow the same pattern: Vocal Shewa (or Hateph vowel) in the first syllable and Qamets in the second syllable.

נֶ֫פֶשׁ	life	➢	נְפָשׁוֹת	lives
חֶ֫רֶב	sword	➢	חֲרָבוֹת	swords
בֹּ֫קֶר	morning	➢	בְּקָרִים	mornings
נַ֫עַר	boy	➢	נְעָרִים	boys

4. **Geminate Nouns**. Nouns of this type have only two root consonants (biconsonantal), as in עַם or חֹק. Originally, however, these nouns had three consonants, and the second and third consonants were identical (e.g., עמם or חקק). In the plural, the original geminate consonant reappears as a Daghesh Forte in the second root letter.

עַם	people	➢	עַמִּים	peoples (עמם)
חֵץ	arrow	➢	חִצִּים	arrows (חצץ)
חֹק	statute	➢	חֻקִּים	statutes (חקק)
יָם	sea	➢	יַמִּים	seas (ימם)

Note, however, that not all biconsonantal nouns were originally geminate nouns. For example, the nouns אָב (father), בֵּן (son), and שֵׁם (name) are biconsonantal but *not* geminate. When these nouns pluralize, there is no Daghesh Forte: אָבוֹת (fathers), בָּנִים (sons), and שֵׁמוֹת (names).

5. **Irregular Nouns**. A number of high frequency nouns are irregular and, therefore, unpredictable in their pluralization.

אִישׁ	man	➢	אֲנָשִׁים	men
אִשָּׁה	woman	➢	נָשִׁים	women
עִיר	city	➢	עָרִים	cities
אָב	father	➢	אָבוֹת	fathers
בַּ֫יִת	house	➢	בָּתִּים	houses
בַּת	daughter	➢	בָּנוֹת	daughters
בֵּן	son	➢	בָּנִים	sons
יוֹם	day	➢	יָמִים	days

DEFINITE ARTICLE

Morphology

The definite article may be prefixed directly to a noun, adjective, demonstrative adjective, or participle. The basic spelling of the article consists of the consonant ה vocalized with Pathach (short a) followed by a Daghesh Forte in the first consonant of the word to which it is prefixed, as in הַסּוּס (*the* horse). It is important to note that the prefixing of the definite article to a word with Daghesh Forte creates a closed syllable.

1. **Basic Spelling**. As stated above, the basic spelling of the article consists of three parts: ה-Pathach-Daghesh Forte.

מִזְבֵּחַ	an altar	➢	הַמִּזְבֵּחַ	the altar
סוּס	a horse	➢	הַסּוּס	the horse
מָקוֹם	a place	➢	הַמָּקוֹם	the place
לֵב	a heart	➢	הַלֵּב	the heart

2. ***Begadkephat* Letters**. When the article is prefixed to a word beginning with a *begadkephat* consonant, the Daghesh Lene in the *begadkephat* consonant is replaced by a Daghesh Forte, creating a closed syllable.

בַּיִת	a house	➢	הַבַּיִת	the house
דֶּרֶךְ	a road	➢	הַדֶּרֶךְ	the road
תּוֹרָה	a law	➢	הַתּוֹרָה	the law
כֹּהֵן	priest	➢	הַכֹּהֵן	the priest

3. **Initial יְ and מְ**. Words that begin with יְ or מְ may give up the Daghesh Forte that is associated with the article. This is the phenomenon known as *sqnmlwy*. Note that the Pathach of the article will *not* reduce in the propretonic position.

יְלָדִים	boys	➢	הַיְלָדִים	the boys
מְרַגְּלִים	spies	➢	הַמְרַגְּלִים	the spies
יְרִיעָה	curtain	➢	הַיְרִיעָה	the curtain
מְגִלָּה	scroll	➢	הַמְגִלָּה	the scroll

4. **Gutturals and Compensatory Lengthening**. With most words that begin with a guttural consonant, the Daghesh Forte of the article is rejected and the Pathach (short a) lengthens to Qamets (long a). In this way, the article "compensates" for the loss of the Daghesh Forte.

אִישׁ	a man	➢	הָאִישׁ	the man
אִשָּׁה	a woman	➢	הָאִשָּׁה	the woman
רֹאשׁ	a head	➢	הָרֹאשׁ	the head
עִיר	a city	➢	הָעִיר	the city

5. **Gutturals and Virtual Doubling**. When the gutturals ה or ח are the first consonant of a word, the rejection of the Daghesh Forte may result in what is called virtual doubling. Virtual doubling is the rejection of the Daghesh Forte without the lengthening of Pathach. In other words, there is *no* Daghesh Forte and *no* lengthening of the Pathach vowel.

הֵיכָל	temple	➢	הַהֵיכָל	the temple
הוֹד	majesty	➢	הַהוֹד	the majesty
חוֹמָה	wall	➢	הַחוֹמָה	the wall
חֹשֶׁךְ	darkness	➢	הַחֹשֶׁךְ	the darkness

6. **Gutturals and Irregular Seghol**. Before nouns that begin with an unaccented הָ, עָ, or חָ (חָ may also be accented), the article may appear with Seghol and without Daghesh Forte.

הָרִים	mountains	➢	הֶהָרִים	the mountains
עָרִים	city	➢	הֶעָרִים	the cities
חָצֵר	courtyard	➢	הֶחָצֵר	the courtyard
עָנָן	cloud	➢	הֶעָנָן	the cloud

Syntax

There are four types of definite nouns in Hebrew. The most common definite nouns are those occurring with the definite article. Proper nouns (Egypt), nouns with possessive pronouns (*your* book), and construct nouns with a definite absolute noun are also considered to be definite.[1]

In general, the Hebrew definite article functions much like the English definite article, making an indefinite noun definite. There are, however, several additional uses of the definite article worth noting.

---

1. In the example מַלְכֵי הָאָ֫רֶץ (the kings of the earth), the construct noun מַלְכֵי is considered definite because the absolute noun to which it is joined (הָאָ֫רֶץ) is definite.

1. **Demonstrative Adjective**. The article can be used like a demonstrative adjective (this, that).

אָנֹכִי מְצַוְּךָ הַיּוֹם

I am commanding you *this* day.

2. **Vocative**. The article can be used on names or titles when a speaker is referring directly to the person (usually translated "O king," "O man," "O LORD," etc.).

וַיִּקְרָא לֵאמֹר הַמֶּלֶךְ

And he called saying, "*O* king."

3. **Superlative**. The article can be employed to indicate the superlative use of adjectives (good/best or upright/most upright).

הַטּוֹב וְהַיָּשָׁר

the *best* and the *most* upright

4. **Possessive**. The article can, at times, be used like a possessive pronoun (my, his, her, your, etc.).

וְלָקַח דָּוִד הַכִּנּוֹר

And David took *his* harp.

5. **Indefinite Article**. Hebrew has no indefinite article. However, the Hebrew word for "one," אֶחָד (ms) and אַחַת (fs), may be used like the English indefinite article: אִישׁ אֶחָד (*a* man) or אִשָּׁה אַחַת (*a* woman).

CONJUNCTION וְ

Morphology

The conjunction וְ may be prefixed directly to any Hebrew word. The basic spelling of this conjunction consists of the consonant ו with Vocal Shewa, as in וְסוּס (*and* a horse).

1. **Basic Spelling**. Before most consonants, the conjunction will appear as וְ (with Vocal Shewa).

וְאִשָּׁה	and a woman
וְהָאִשָּׁה	and the woman
וְאִישׁ	and a man
וְהָאִישׁ	and the man

2. **Spelled as Shureq**. There are two circumstances in which the conjunction is spelled as וּ (Shureq): (a) when prefixed to the consonants ב or מ or פ (*bump* rule); and (b) when prefixed to words beginning with Vocal Shewa. This second situation is the exception to the First Rule of Shewa.

   Examples when prefixed to *bump* consonants:

וּבֵין	and between
וּמִשְׁפָּט	and a judgment

   Examples when prefixed to consonants with Vocal Shewa:

וּסְפָרִים	and books
וּשְׁמוּאֵל	and Samuel

3. **Spelled with a Short Vowel**. When prefixed to consonants with one of the Hateph vowels, the conjunction is spelled with the corresponding short vowel of the Hateph vowel. This spelling follows the Second Rule of Shewa.

וַאֲנָשִׁים	and men
וֶאֱמֶת	and truth
וָחֳלִי	and sickness

4. **Spelled with Qamets**. The conjunction may be spelled with Qamets before monosyllabic words and certain words accented on the first syllable. This spelling follows the vowel rule that open pretonic syllable take long vowels. Note, however, that this spelling of the conjunction does *not* always follow the rule.

   Examples when prefixed to monosyllabic words:

וָצֹאן	and a flock
וָדֹר	and a generation

   Examples when prefixed to words accented on the first syllable:

וָלָ֫יְלָה	and night
וָאָ֫רֶץ	and earth

5. **Spelled with Hireq Yod**. If the conjunction is prefixed to a word that begins with the syllable יְ (Yod with Vocal Shewa), then these two syllables contract to וִי (Waw with Hireq Yod): וְיְהוּדָה becomes וִיְהוּדָה which finally becomes וִיהוּדָה.

This spelling follows the exception to the First Rule of Shewa.

6. **Spelled with Tsere**. When אֱלֹהִים (God) occurs with the conjunction, it is spelled וֵאלֹהִים (Waw with Tsere): וְאֱלֹהִים becomes וֶאלֹהִים (Aleph becomes quiescent) which finally becomes וֵאלֹהִים (compensatory lengthening of Seghol to Tsere).

Syntax

The conjunction וְ joins groups of words, phrases, and clauses.

1. **Conjunctive**. The conjunction וְ may be used to join related nouns in a series. The translation "and" is best suited for this usage.

    בְּרֵאשִׁית בָּרָא אֱלֹהִים אֵת הַשָּׁמַיִם וְאֵת הָאָרֶץ

    In the beginning, God created
    the heavens *and* the earth.

2. **Alternative**. The conjunction וְ may be used to join alternative nouns in a series. The translation "or" is best suited for this usage.

    וְלֹא אוֹשִׁיעֵם בְּקֶשֶׁת וּבְחֶרֶב וּבְמִלְחָמָה

    I will not save them with bow,
    or with sword, *or* with war.

3. **Parenthetical/Circumstantial**. The conjunction וְ may be used to introduce a clause with some explanatory or circumstantial information that is important for understanding the narrative.

וַיְהִי כְּהַיּוֹם הַזֶּה וַיָּבֹא הַבַּיְתָה לַעֲשׂוֹת מְלַאכְתּוֹ
וְאֵין אִישׁ מֵאַנְשֵׁי הַבַּיִת שָׁם בַּבָּיִת

And on this day, he went into the house
to do his work *and* none of the household
servants were there in the house.

4. **Contrastive**. The conjunction וְ may be used to introduce a clause that presents information in contrast to the information in the preceding clause or clauses. The translation "but" is best suited for this usage.

וַיִּשַׁע יְהוָה אֶל־הֶבֶל וְאֶל־מִנְחָתוֹ
וְאֶל־קַיִן וְאֶל־מִנְחָתוֹ לֹא שָׁעָה

Yahweh looked favorably on Abel
and his offering *but* on Cain and his
offering he did not look favorably.

5. **Introductory**. The conjunction וְ may begin a new narrative or introduce a new idea or theme within a narrative.

וְהַנָּחָשׁ הָיָה עָרוּם מִכֹּל חַיַּת הַשָּׂדֶה
אֲשֶׁר עָשָׂה יְהוָה אֱלֹהִים

Now the serpent was more crafty than
any of the creatures that
Yahweh God had made.

PREPOSITIONS

Basic Grammar

Prepositions are used to describe relationships between words. These relationships can be **spatial** as in *under* the book, *on* the book, *over* the book. These relationships can also be **temporal** as in *before* class, *during* class, *after* class. Many other relationships also exist.

Prepositions introduce prepositional phrases. A **prepositional phrase** contains a preposition, the object of the preposition, and any words that modify the object. With the example, "in the good book," the object of the preposition is "the good book." Technically speaking, though, the object is "book" with "the" and "good" modifying the object.

A prepositional phrase can modify both nouns and verbs. When a prepositional phrase modifies a verb, it is **adverbial**. In the example, "The student read the book *after school*," the prepositional phrase "after school" modifies the verb "read," indicating when the student read. Thus, the prepositional phrase is adverbial.

When a prepositional phrase modifies a noun, it is **adjectival**. In the example, "The student read the book *with Hebrew letters*," the prepositional phrase "with Hebrew letters" modifies the noun "book," describing a particular characteristic of the book.

Types of Hebrew Prepositions

In biblical Hebrew there are four types of prepositions: inseparable, Maqqef, independent, and compound prepositions.

1. **Inseparable Prepositions**. These prepositions are prefixed directly to their objects and never occur independently. There are three inseparable prepositions: בְּ (in, by, with), לְ (to, for), and כְּ (like, as, according to).

   בְּשָׂדֶה *in* a field
   לְנַ֫עַר *for* a young man
   כְּמֶ֫לֶךְ *like* a king

2. **Maqqef Prepositions**. Prepositions of this type are almost always joined to their objects by a raised horizontal stroke called Maqqef. Common examples include עַל־ (on, upon, concerning), אֶל־ (to, toward), עַד־ (until, as far as) and מִן־ (from).

   עַל־הָאֶ֫בֶן *upon* the stone
   אֶל־הַהֵיכָל *to* the temple
   עַד־הַנָּהָר *as far as* the river
   מִן־הָאָ֫רֶץ *from* the land

3. **Independent Prepositions**. These prepositions are not prefixed to other words, nor are they normally joined to other words by Maqqef. They are independent.

תַּ֫חַת הָעֵץ *under* the tree
אַחַר הַמַּבּוּל *after* the flood
בֵּין הַמַּיִם *between* the water(s)

4. **Compound Prepositions**. Some Hebrew prepositions are formed by combining two different prepositions, or a preposition and a noun, in order to make a new preposition.

The following compound prepositions are created by combining the preposition מִן (from) with another preposition.

מֵעַל from upon (מִן + עַל)
מִתַּ֫חַת from under (מִן + תַּ֫חַת)
מֵאֵת from with (מִן + אֵת)

The following compound prepositions are created by combining a preposition with a noun.

עַל־דְּבַר on account of (עַל + דָּבָר)
בְּתוֹךְ in the midst of (בְּ + תָּ֫וֶךְ)
מִתּוֹךְ from the midst of (מִן + תָּ֫וֶךְ)

Several compound prepositions are formed by combining a preposition with the noun פָּנֶה (face) in the masculine plural construct (פְּנֵי).

לִפְנֵי before, in the presence of (לְ + פָּנִים)
מִפְּנֵי away from, out from, from the presence of, from before, on account of, because of (מִן + פָּנִים)

מִלִּפְנֵי away from, from before, from the presence of, on account of

(מִן + לְ + פָּנִים)

עַל־פְּנֵי in the face of, in the sight of, in front of, before, up against, opposite to

(עַל־ + פָּנִים)

The Spelling of Inseparable Prepositions

1. Before most consonants, the inseparable prepositions are spelled with Vocal Shewa.

   בְּשָׂדֶה in a field

   כְּמֶלֶךְ like a king

   לְנַעַר for a young man

2. Before consonants with Vocal Shewa, the inseparable prepositions are spelled with Hireq (First Rule of Shewa).

   לִנְבִיאִים for prophets

   לִבְרִית for a covenant

3. Before a Hateph vowel, the inseparable prepositions take the corresponding short vowel of the Hateph vowel (Second Rule of Shewa).

   כַּאֲנָשִׁים like men

   בֶּאֱמֶת in truth

   לָחֳלִי for sickness

4. In nouns with the definite article, the vowel and Daghesh Forte of the article are retained but the consonant of the preposition replaces the ה of the article.

בַּשָּׂדֶה in the field
בָּאֵשׁ in the fire
לַנַּ֫עַר for the boy
כַּמֶּ֫לֶךְ like the king

The Preposition מִן

The preposition מִן may occur either as a Maqqef preposition or as an inseparable preposition.

1. The preposition מִן may be joined to its object by Maqqef.

מִן־הַבַּיִת from the house
מִן־הַמַּלְכָּה from the queen

2. The preposition מִן can also occur as an inseparable preposition. When this happens, the נ of the preposition assimilates into the first consonant of the noun to which it is prefixed. It is represented by Daghesh Forte in that first consonant.

מִמֶּ֫לֶךְ from a king
מִצִּיּוֹן from Zion

a. When מִן is inseparably prefixed to a word beginning with a *begadkephat* consonant, the Daghesh Lene of the *begadkephat* consonant becomes a Daghesh Forte.

מִבַּ֫יִת from a house

מִכָּל from all

b. When מִן is inseparably prefixed to a word beginning with a guttural consonant, the guttural rejects the Daghesh Forte of the assimilating נ and the Hireq of the Preposition lengthens to Tsere. This is **compensatory lengthening**.

מֵאִישׁ from a man

מֵעִיר from a city

c. When מִן is inseparably prefixed to a word beginning with ח, the Daghesh Forte is often rejected by the guttural but without the compensatory lengthening of Hireq. This is **virtual doubling**. In some instances, however, compensatory lengthening will occur.

מִחוּץ from outside (with virtual doubling)

מֵחֶ֫רֶב from a sword (with compensatory lengthening)

d. When מִן is prefixed to words with the definite article, the ה of the article is retained. It does not drop out as it would with the regular inseparable prepositions.

מֵהָאָ֫רֶץ from thc land

מֵהַיּוֹם from the day

Special Uses of the Preposition מִן

1. **Comparative Use**. In English, adjectives are used to express the comparative and superlative ideas: big becomes bigger (comparative) or biggest (superlative) and good becomes better (comparative) or best (superlative). In Hebrew, the preposition מִן is often used to indicate the comparative or "better than" idea.

   טוֹבָה חָכְמָה מִזָּהָב

   Wisdom is *better than* gold.

2. **Superlative Use**. The preposition מִן may be used with כֹּל (all, each, every) in the formation of a superlative מִכֹּל, literally "from every."

   עָרוּם מִכֹּל חַיַּת הַשָּׂדֶה

   the most clever living thing of the field

3. **Partitive Use**. The partitive use of מִן is the way that Hebrew expresses a part or portion of something.

   מִפְּרִי

   some (of the) fruit

   מֵהָאֲנָשִׁים

   some of the men

ADJECTIVES

Adjective Paradigm

Hebrew adjectives inflect (change their form) in order to indicate gender and number. They are inflected in four forms: masculine singular and masculine plural, feminine singular and feminine plural. The inflectional endings for adjectives are the same endings that appear with nouns. The Hebrew adjective טוֹב (good) is inflected below.

	Masculine	Feminine
Singular	טוֹב	טוֹבָה
Plural	טוֹבִים	טוֹבוֹת

Paradigm Notes

1. The lexical (dictionary) form for any adjective is the *masculine singular* form.
2. Hebrew adjectives must agree in gender and number with the nouns they modify.
3. Adjectives that are plural in form are singular in English translation value. In other words, they do not translate with any kind of plural meaning.
4. Unlike טוֹב, most adjectives undergo vowel changes when the inflectional endings are added. These changes are detailed below.

Adjectival Inflection

When an adjective is inflected for gender and number, the accent and syllable structure of that adjective may change. Changes of this type will frequently impact the vocalization (vowels) of the inflected forms. Knowing the types of changes that occur is essential for identification and translation.

1. **No Change**. Certain adjectives, like the monosyllabic adjective טוֹב, do not change with the addition of inflectional endings.

	Masculine	Feminine
Singular	טוֹב	טוֹבָה
Plural	טוֹבִים	טוֹבוֹת

2. **Propretonic Reduction**. With adjectives consisting of two syllables, the addition of inflectional endings causes the originally open pretonic syllable to become propretonic. Thus, the original (changeable) long vowel in the open syllable will reduce to Vocal Shewa (or Hateph Pathach with gutturals).

	Masculine	Feminine
Singular	גָּדוֹל	גְּדוֹלָה
Plural	גְּדוֹלִים	גְּדוֹלוֹת

	Masculine	Feminine
Singular	חָכָם	חֲכָמָה
Plural	חֲכָמִים	חֲכָמוֹת

3. **Geminate Adjectives**. Like Geminate nouns, Geminate adjectives, such as רַב (many), will take a Daghesh Forte in the second consonant with the addition of inflectional endings. The Daghesh Forte in the inflected forms closes the first syllable and preserves the short vowel.

	Masculine	Feminine
Singular	רַב	רַבָּה
Plural	רַבִּים	רַבּוֹת

Geminate adjectives like רַע (evil), with a guttural Geminate consonant, cannot take Daghesh Forte. Because gutturals reject Daghesh Forte, the Pathach under the first root letter lengthens to Qamets (compensatory lengthening).

	Masculine	Feminine
Singular	רַע	רָעָה
Plural	רָעִים	רָעוֹת

4. **Adjectives Ending in Seghol He**. Both nouns and adjectives that end with Seghol He are masculine, as in קָשֶׁה (difficult). When adjectives of this type inflect, the Seghol He drops off before the inflectional ending.

	Masculine	Feminine
Singular	קָשֶׁה	קָשָׁה
Plural	קָשִׁים	קָשׁוֹת

Syntax

Adjectival usage falls into three categories: attributive, predicative, and substantive.

1. **Attributive**. When an adjective modifies a noun, it is being used attributively. In Hebrew, attributive adjectives follow the nouns they modify. The modifying adjective must agree with the noun in gender, number, and definiteness.

הַמֶּ֫לֶךְ הַטּוֹב	the *good* king
הַנְּבִיאִים הָרִאשֹׁנִים	the *former* prophets
חֲשֵׁכָה גְדֹלָה	a *great* darkness
מַמְלָכוֹת גְּדֹלוֹת	*great* kingdoms

2. **Predicative**. The predicative adjective asserts (predicates) something about a noun. In English, a form of the verb "to be" (followed by the predicate adjective) is used to indicate the predicative relationship. In Hebrew, the predicative adjective will agree with the noun in gender and number but not in definiteness. The predicate adjective never takes the definite article and may either precede or follow the noun.

הַיּוֹם גָּדוֹל	the day *is great*
הַדְּבָרִים עַתִּיקִים	the words *are ancient*
הָרָעָב כָּבֵד	the famine *was severe*
כָּבֵד הָרָעָב	the famine *was severe*
טוֹב הָעֵץ	the tree *is good*

When a Hebrew noun is indefinite, only context will determine whether an adjective is attributive or predicative.

אָב זָקֵן	a father *is old* or an *old* father
זֶבַח־גָּדוֹל	a sacrifice *is great* or a *great* sacrifice

3. **Substantive**. Adjectives of this type are used independently as nouns. In such cases, there will be no noun for the adjective to modify.

קַח־נָא אֶת־בִּנְךָ אֶת־יְחִידְךָ

Take now your son, your *only one*.

דִּבְרֵי חֲכָמִים

words of *wise men*

כְּאַחַד הַנְּבָלִים בְּיִשְׂרָאֵל

like one of the *foolish* (men) in Israel

INDEPENDENT PERSONAL PRONOUNS

Morphology

These personal pronouns are labeled "independent" because they stand alone and are not prefixed or suffixed to another word. Personal pronouns can be first, second, or third person and either singular or plural. The second and third person pronouns have both masculine and feminine forms. First person pronouns are common, meaning that they may refer to either masculine or feminine nouns (they are not inflected for gender).

	Singular		Plural	
3 Masculine	הוּא	he, it	הֵ֫מָּה/הֵם	they
3 Feminine	הִיא/הִוא	she, it	הֵ֫נָּה/הֵן	they
2 Masculine	אַתָּה	you	אַתֶּם	you
2 Feminine	אַתְּ	you	אַתֵּ֫נָה	you
1 Common	אֲנִי/אָנֹכִי	I	אֲנַ֫חְנוּ	we

Syntax

Independent personal pronouns are subjective, meaning they are used as the subject of a verb, never as the object of a verb. Personal pronouns may also appear as the subject of a verbless clause. For these reasons, they are sometimes called "subject" pronouns.

In the following examples, independent personal pronouns appear as the subject of **verbal clauses**.

וְהוּא יִמְשָׁל־בָּךְ

And *he* will rule over you.

וְאַתָּה תָּבוֹא אֶל־אֲבֹתֶיךָ בְּשָׁלוֹם

And *you* will go to your fathers in peace.

אֲנִי לְקַחְתִּיךָ מִן־הַנָּוֶה

I took you from the pasture.

In the next set of examples, independent personal pronouns appear as the subject of **verbless clauses**.

אַתֶּם עַם־קְשֵׁה־עֹרֶף

You are a stiff necked people.

אֲנַחְנוּ בְּנֵי אִישׁ־אֶחָד

We are the sons of one man.

הוּא יְהוָה אֱלֹהֵינוּ

He is Yahweh our God.

Finally, note that the third person pronoun (singular or plural) may be used as a **copula** and translated with a form of the verb "to be" in English.

וְיוֹסֵף הוּא הַשַּׁלִּיט עַל־הָאָרֶץ

And Joseph *was* the ruler over the land.

יְהוָה אֱלֹהֶיךָ אֵשׁ אֹכְלָה הוּא

Yahweh your God *is* a consuming fire.

אֵלֶּה הֵם בְּנֵי יִשְׁמָעֵאל

These *are* the sons of Ishmael.

DEMONSTRATIVES

Morphology

The English demonstratives are "this," "these," "that," and "those." They may be used either as adjectives (this man, those women) or as pronouns (this is the man, those are the women). Demonstratives increase the level of a word's specificity beyond that of the definite article. The level of specific reference increases from "a man," to "the man," to "this man." Hebrew demonstratives function like English demonstratives.

	Singular		Plural	
Masculine	זֶה	this	אֵ֫לֶּה	these
Feminine	זאת	this	אֵ֫לֶּה	these
Masculine	הוּא	that	הֵ֫מָּה/הֵם	those
Feminine	הִיא	that	הֵ֫נָּה/הֵן	those

Notes

1. The masculine and feminine singular forms הוּא and הִיא are identical to the third person masculine and feminine independent personal pronouns. In most instances where ambiguity exists, the larger context of the sentence will enable you to make the correct choice.

2. The demonstrative אֵ֫לֶּה (these) is both masculine and feminine plural. The designation for this phenomenon is "common."

Syntax

Hebrew demonstratives may be used either as adjectives (this man, those women) or as pronouns (this is the man, those are the women).

1. **Demonstrative Adjectives**. When a Hebrew demonstrative is functioning as an adjective, it will follow the noun it modifies and agree in gender, number, and definiteness. This is just like the attributive use of adjectives.

הַיּוֹם הַזֶּה	*this* day
הָאָ֫רֶץ הַזֹּאת	*this* land
הַדְּבָרִים הָאֵ֫לֶּה	*these* words
הַתּוֹעֵבֹת הָאֵ֫לֶּה	*these* abominations

2. **Demonstrative Pronouns**. When a Hebrew demonstrative is functioning as a pronoun, it will precede the noun and agree in gender and number *but not definiteness*. This is just like the predicative use of adjectives.

זֶה הַדָּבָר	*This* is the word.
זֹאת הַתּוֹרָה	*This* is the law.
אֵ֫לֶּה הַמִּשְׁפָּטִים	*These* are the judgments.
אֵ֫לֶּה הַמִּצְוֹת	*These* are the commandments.

RELATIVE PRONOUNS

The Relative Pronoun אֲשֶׁר

The major relative pronouns in English are "who," "whom," "whose," "that," and "which." A relative pronoun introduces a relative clause that modifies a noun. A relative clause is composed of the relative pronoun and the clause that it introduces. In the sentence "happy is the person who studies Hebrew," the clause "who studies Hebrew" is a relative clause modifying the noun "person." In Hebrew, the word אֲשֶׁר functions as the relative pronoun. The form of this word never changes. In the following examples, you will notice that when אֲשֶׁר functions as a relative pronoun introducing a relative clause, it immediately follows the noun it is modifying.

הָעֵץ אֲשֶׁר בְּתוֹךְ־הַגָּן

the tree *that* (is) in the middle of the garden

הֶהָרִים אֲשֶׁר־תַּ֫חַת הַשָּׁמָ֫יִם

the mountains *that* (are) under the heavens

הַמֶּ֫לֶךְ אֲשֶׁר בְּחַרְתֶּם

the king *whom* you chose

דָּוִד אֲשֶׁר בְּבֵית יְהוָה

David, *who* (is) in the house of Yahweh

The Relative Pronoun שֶׁ

The relative pronoun שֶׁ occurs 142 times in the Hebrew Bible. It appears with greatest frequency in Ecclesiastes (70 times), Song of Songs (32 times), and Psalms (21 times). This relative pronoun is prefixed to the first word of the relative clause that it introduces. When prefixed, a Daghesh Forte is added to the first consonant of the word to which it is prefixed, much like the definite article (שֶׁמְּצָאתִי, "who found me"). If the word to which it is prefixed begins with a guttural consonant, the Daghesh Forte will not appear and the Seghol *does not* lengthen (שֶׁעִמָּהֶם, "who are with them"). In other words, compensatory lengthening does not occur in this instance.[1]

יְהוָה שֶׁהָיָה לָנוּ

Yahweh *who* was for us

הָאָדָם שֶׁיָּבוֹא אַחֲרֵי הַמֶּלֶךְ

The man *who* comes after the king

וְעָשִׂיתָ לִּי אוֹת שָׁאַתָּה מְדַבֵּר עִמִּי

Then you will perform a sign for me
that you are speaking with me.

---

1. In addition to the spelling שֶׁ (134 times), the spellings שַׁ (6 times), שָׁ (1 time), and שְׁ (1 time) also occur.

INTERROGATIVE PRONOUNS

Interrogative pronouns are used to ask a question. These pronouns do not inflect for gender or number.[1]

1. **The Interrogative מָה (what?).** In addition to מָה, this interrogative is also spelled מַה and מֶה (behaving much like the definite article). When spelled as מַה, a Daghesh Forte will usually appear in the first consonant of the following word (unless that consonant is a guttural).

מַה־שְּׁמוֹ	*What* (is) his name?
מֶה־עָשִׂיתָ	*What* have you done?
מָה הַחֲלוֹם הַזֶּה	*What* (is) this dream?

2. **The Interrogative מִי (who?).** The vocalization of מִי is stable. It does not change.

מִי־אַתָּה	*Who* (are) you?
מִי־הָאִישׁ הַזֶּה	*Who* (is) this man?
מִי הָאֲנָשִׁים הָאֵלֶּה	*Who* (are) these men?

3. **The Interrogative לָמָה or לָ֫מָּה (why?).**

אֵלִי אֵלִי לָמָה עֲזַבְתָּנִי
My God, my God, *why* have you forsaken me?

לָ֫מָּה תַעֲשֶׂה כֹה לַעֲבָדֶיךָ
Why are you doing thus to your servants?

1. Hebrew also employs the interrogative particle הֲ in order to ask questions. See the section on Particles.

4. **The Interrogative אֵיךְ or אֵיכָה (how?).**

וְאֵיךְ אֶעֱשֶׂה הָרָעָה הַגְּדֹלָה הַזֹּאת
How could I do this great evil?

אֵיכָה נֵדַע אֶת־הַדָּבָר
How can we know the word?

5. **The Interrogative אֵי or אַיֵּה (where?).**

אֵי הֶבֶל אָחִיךָ
Where is Abel your brother?

אַיֵּה שָׂרָה אִשְׁתֶּךָ
Where is Sarah your wife?

PRONOMINAL SUFFIXES

Morphology

In Hebrew, there are two sets of pronominal suffixes: Type 1 (including alternate Type 1) and Type 2. Both types have the same possessive and objective translation values. As suffixes, these pronouns are attached to the end of a word.

	Type 1	Alternate Type 1	Type 2	Translation
3ms	וֹ	הוּ	ָיו	his (its)/him (it)
3fs	ָהּ	הָ	ֶיהָ	her (its)/her (it)
2ms	ךָ		ֶיךָ	your/you
2fs	ךְ		ַיִךְ	your/you
1cs	ִי	נִי	ַי	my/me
3mp	הֶם	ָם	ֵיהֶם	their/them
3fp	הֶן	ָן	ֵיהֶן	their/them
2mp	כֶם		ֵיכֶם	your/you
2fp	כֶן		ֵיכֶן	your/you
1cp	נוּ		ֵינוּ	our/us

Notes on Pronominal Suffixes

1. Pronominal suffixes appear on nouns, verbs, prepositions, and a variety of Hebrew particles. When appearing on nouns, these pronouns are **possessive**, as in "his," "her," or "my." When appearing on verbs, prepositions, or particles, they are **objective**, as in "him," "her," or "me."

2. With few exceptions, Type 1 suffixes occur with singular nouns, verbs, and Hebrew particles. Type 2 suffixes occur with plural nouns. Prepositions prefer either Type 1 or Type 2 pronominal suffixes.

3. Pronominal suffixes have person, gender, and number. With regard to gender, second and third person pronouns have both masculine and feminine forms. First person pronouns are common, meaning that they may refer to either masculine or feminine nouns (they are not inflected for gender).

4. Note the dot in the הּ of the Type 1 3fs suffix (ּהּ). This is not a Daghesh Lene or a Daghesh Forte. The Daghesh Lene occurs only in a *begadkephat* consonant and the Daghesh Forte cannot occur in the gutturals or ר. This dot in a final הּ is called **Mappiq** and frequently marks the 3fs suffix.

Pronominal Suffixes on Masculine Nouns

Singular nouns use Type 1 suffixes and plural nouns use Type 2 suffixes. When pronominal suffixes are added to masculine plural nouns, the masculine plural ending (ִים) is dropped. With the absence of this ending, a masculine noun is recognizable as plural only by the use of Type 2 pronominal suffixes.[1]

	Singular Noun Type 1	Plural Noun Type 2
3ms	סוּסוֹ	סוּסָיו
3fs	סוּסָהּ	סוּסֶ֫יהָ
2ms	סוּסְךָ	סוּסֶ֫יךָ
2fs	סוּסֵךְ	סוּסַ֫יִךְ
1cs	סוּסִי	סוּסַי
3mp	סוּסָם	סוּסֵיהֶם
3fp	סוּסָן	סוּסֵיהֶן
2mp	סוּסְכֶם	סוּסֵיכֶם
2fp	סוּסְכֶן	סוּסֵיכֶן
1cp	סוּסֵ֫נוּ	סוּסֵ֫ינוּ

1. Masculine nouns ending in Seghol He, as in שָׂדֶה, drop this final vowel letter before adding a pronominal suffix (e.g., שָׂדְךָ, "your field.").

Pronominal Suffixes on Feminine Nouns

Feminine nouns also take Type 1 suffixes in the singular and Type 2 suffixes in the plural. When a feminine singular noun ending in Qamets He (as in תּוֹרָה) receives a pronominal suffix, the ה is replaced by ת. In other words, the feminine singular noun תּוֹרָה becomes תּוֹרַת before receiving a pronominal suffix.

	Singular Noun Type 1	Plural Noun Type 2
3ms	תּוֹרָתוֹ	תּוֹרוֹתָיו
3fs	תּוֹרָתָהּ	תּוֹרוֹתֶ֫יהָ
2ms	תּוֹרָתְךָ	תּוֹרוֹתֶ֫יךָ
2fs	תּוֹרָתֵךְ	תּוֹרוֹתַ֫יִךְ
1cs	תּוֹרָתִי	תּוֹרוֹתַי
3mp	תּוֹרָתָם	תּוֹרוֹתֵיהֶם
3fp	תּוֹרָתָן	תּוֹרוֹתֵיהֶן
2mp	תּוֹרַתְכֶם	תּוֹרוֹתֵיכֶם
2fp	תּוֹרַתְכֶן	תּוֹרוֹתֵיכֶן
1cp	תּוֹרָתֵ֫נוּ	תּוֹרוֹתֵ֫ינוּ

Pronominal Suffixes on Monosyllabic Nouns

Certain singular monosyllabic nouns add Hireq Yod to their stem before a pronominal suffix. The addition of Hireq Yod to singular nouns may cause them to be confused with plural nouns having Type 2 suffixes. With regard to consonants, both paradigms are identical. The singular noun paradigm, however, has Hireq Yod throughout. The plural noun paradigm varies its vowel, but never has Hireq Yod.

	Singular Noun Type 1	Plural Noun Type 2
3ms	אָחִיו	אֶחָיו
3fs	אָחִ֫יהָ	אַחֶ֫יהָ
2ms	אָחִ֫יךָ	אַחֶ֫יךָ
2fs	אָחִ֫יךְ	אַחַ֫יִךְ
1cs	אָחִי	אַחַי
3mp	אֲחִיהֶם	אֲחֵיהֶם
3fp	אֲחִיהֶן	אֲחֵיהֶן
2mp	אֲחִיכֶם	אֲחֵיכֶם
2fp	אֲחִיכֶן	אֲחֵיכֶן
1cp	אָחִ֫ינוּ	אַחֵ֫ינוּ

Pronominal Suffixes on Prepositions

Pronominal suffixes on prepositions are objective, functioning as the object of the preposition as in "to *him*," "for *her*," or "with *me*." Certain prepositions take Type 1 suffixes and others take Type 2 suffixes. The translation value is the same for both types. By way of illustration, the inseparable preposition לְ takes Type 1 suffixes. The preposition עַל takes Type 2 suffixes.

	Preposition לְ Type 1	Preposition עַל Type 2
3ms	לוֹ	עָלָיו
3fs	לָהּ	עָלֶיהָ
2ms	לְךָ	עָלֶיךָ
2fs	לָךְ	עָלַיִךְ
1cs	לִי	עָלַי
3mp	לָהֶם	עֲלֵיהֶם
3fp	לָהֶן	עֲלֵיהֶן
2mp	לָכֶם	עֲלֵיכֶם
2fp	לָכֶן	עֲלֵיכֶן
1cp	לָנוּ	עָלֵינוּ

Pronominal Suffixes on כְּ and מִן

These two prepositions are spelled differently when pronominal suffixes are added. With the preposition כְּ, the forms with singular and 1cp suffixes exhibit a longer, alternate spelling of the preposition (כְּמוֹ). With the preposition מִן, the forms with singular and 1cp suffixes also exhibit a longer, alternate spelling of the preposition (מִמֶּ). Note the presence of alternate endings throughout the paradigm with מִן.

	Preposition כְּ Type 1 (alt)	Preposition מִן Type 1 (alt)
3ms	כָּמֹ֫והוּ	מִמֶּ֫נּוּ
3fs	כָּמֹ֫והָ	מִמֶּ֫נָּה
2ms	כָּמֹ֫וךָ	מִמְּךָ
2fs	כָּמוֹךְ	מִמֵּךְ
1cs	כָּמֹ֫ונִי	מִמֶּ֫נִּי
3mp	כָּהֶם	מֵהֶם
3fp	כָּהֶן	מֵהֶן
2mp	כָּכֶם	מִכֶּם
2fp	כָּכֶן	מִכֶּן
1cp	כָּמֹ֫ונוּ	מִמֶּ֫נּוּ

Pronominal Suffixes on אֵת/אֶת־

The definite direct object marker אֵת/אֶת־ and the preposition אֵת/אֶת־ (with) share the same lexical form. However, when appearing with a pronominal suffix, these forms are easy to distinguish. The object marker is spelled with Holem (or Seghol) and the preposition is spelled with Hireq and then Daghesh Forte in the ת. These are important distinctions to remember. Both paradigms are listed below for comparison.

	Object Marker Type 1	Preposition Type 2
3ms	אֹתוֹ	אִתּוֹ
3fs	אֹתָהּ	אִתָּהּ
2ms	אֹתְךָ	אִתְּךָ
2fs	אֹתָךְ	אִתָּךְ
1cs	אֹתִי	אִתִּי
3mp	אֹתָם	אִתָּם
3fp	אֹתָן	אִתָּן
2mp	אֶתְכֶם	אִתְּכֶם
2fp	אֶתְכֶן	אִתְּכֶן
1cp	אֹתָ֫נוּ	אִתָּ֫נוּ

Pronominal Suffix as a Resumptive Pronoun

A relative clause, often beginning with אֲשֶׁר, modifies the noun that it follows. In Hebrew, a relative clause may contain a resumptive pronoun. A resumptive pronoun is a pronoun *within* the relative clause that refers back to the noun that the relative clause modifies. In "the king whom you chose *him*," the word "him" is a resumptive pronoun referring back to "king." Similarly, in the sentence "This is the book that I read *it*," the word "it" is a resumptive pronoun referring back to "book." Resumptive pronouns are common in Hebrew. However, they are improper in English, so they should be omitted from English translation.

הַמָּקוֹם אֲשֶׁר אַתָּה עוֹמֵד עָלָיו

the place which you are standing on (*it*)

הַבָּתִּים אֲשֶׁר־יֹאכְלוּ אֹתוֹ בָּהֶם

the houses which they eat it in (*them*)

וַיִּשְׁמְרֵנוּ בְּכָל־הַדֶּרֶךְ אֲשֶׁר הָלַכְנוּ בָהּ

And he guarded us in all the way
that we walked in (*it*).

Pronominal Suffixes with Perfect Verbs

The following chart provides the basic and most frequently attested spellings of pronominal suffixes on Perfect verbs. In this chart, the connecting vowels are included and the suffixes are placed in one of two categories: (1) those attached to Perfect forms ending in a consonant; and (2) those attached to Perfect forms that end in a vowel.

	After Consonant	After Vowel
3ms	וֹ/ו/הוּ/ָ֫הוּ	הוּ/ו
3fs	ָהּ/ָה	הָ
2ms	ךָ/ְךָ/ֲךָ	ךָ
2fs	ָךְ/ֵךְ	ךְ
1cs	ַ֫נִי/ָנִי/נִי	נִי
3mp	ַם/ָם	ם
3fp	ָן	ן
2mp	כֶם	כֶם
2fp		
1cp	נוּ/ָ֫נוּ	נוּ

Pronominal Suffixes with Imperfect (Imperative) Verbs

The following provides the basic and most frequently attested spellings of pronominal suffixes on Imperfect verbs. In this chart, the connecting vowels are included. Note the important category of pronominal suffixes labelled as Nun-suffixes.

	Type 1 Suffixes	Nun-Suffixes
3ms	הוּ/ֵ֫הוּ	ֶ֫נּוּ
3fs	ָהּ/ֶ֫הָ/הָ	ֶ֫נָּה
2ms	ךָ/ְךָ/ֲךָ/ֶךָ	ֶ֫ךָּ
2fs	ךְ/ֵךְ	
1cs	נִי/ַ֫נִי/ֵ֫נִי	ֶ֫נִּי
3mp	ם/ֵם	ם
3fp	ָן	
2mp	ְכֶם	
2fp		
1cp	נוּ/ֵ֫נוּ	ֶ֫נּוּ

CONSTRUCT CHAIN

In Biblical Hebrew, there is no word for "of." Rather, Hebrew expresses the "of" (genitive) relationship between two nouns by what is called the construct chain. This grammatical relationship is created by placing two or more nouns side by side.

קוֹל הָאִישׁ	the voice of the man *or* the man's voice
מֶ֫לֶךְ הָאָ֫רֶץ	the king of the land *or* the land's king
עֶ֫בֶד הַמֶּ֫לֶךְ	the servant of the king *or* the king's servant

Basic Grammar of the Construct Chain

1. The first of two nouns in a construct chain is called the construct noun and is said to be in the **construct state**. The second of the two nouns is called the absolute noun and is said to be in the **absolute state**. The absolute form of a noun is also its lexical form.

2. In a construct chain, there is only **one absolute noun** and the absolute noun is always the last noun in the chain. **Multiple construct nouns** may appear in any construct chain. In instances where multiple construct nouns appear, each construct noun is translated with the key word "of," and they all depend on the absolute noun for definiteness.

3. Construct chains are either entirely definite (the … of the …) or entirely indefinite (a … of a …). The definiteness or indefiniteness of a construct chain is determined by the absolute noun. A construct chain is **definite** if the absolute noun is definite. A construct chain is **indefinite** if the absolute noun is indefinite.[1] The absolute noun is considered definite if: (a) it appears with the definite article; (b) it appears with a pronominal suffix; or (c) it is a proper noun.

4. When two or more nouns appear in construct, no other words or particles may separate them. For this reason, when an adjective modifies either the construct or absolute noun, it must follow the entire chain and agree with the noun it modifies in gender, number, and definiteness.

5. The nouns of a construct chain are sometimes joined by **Maqqef**. The use of the Maqqef indicates that the two joined words form a single accented unit.

6. Although a construct noun cannot take the definite article, a construct noun may appear with one of the inseparable prepositions (בְּ, כְּ, לְ) as in בְּבֵית דָּוִד, meaning "*in* the house of David."

---

1. When two nouns appear together in the "of" or genitive relationship, but the first noun is indefinite and the second noun is definite, a construction with the preposition לְ is used: בֵּן לְיִשַׁי (a son of Jesse) or נָבִיא לַיהוָה (a prophet of Yahweh).

Spelling Changes in the Construct Noun

When a noun appears in the construct state, it surrenders its primary accent to the absolute noun and the entire construct chain is treated as a single accented unit. Because the construct noun surrenders its primary accent, the spelling of a construct noun usually changes from its spelling in the absolute state (lexical form). The vowels of the construct noun will reduce as much as possible, with short vowels appearing in closed syllables and Vocal Shewa (or a Hateph Vowel) appearing in originally open syllables. Changes of this type, and other important spelling changes, are detailed below.

1. **No Change in Spelling**. Singular monosyllabic nouns with an unchangeable long vowel (Holem Waw, Shureq, or Hireq Yod) and singular Segholate nouns exhibit no spelling changes in the construct state.

   קוֹל voice ➢ קוֹל voice of

   שִׁיר song ➢ שִׁיר song of

   מֶ֫לֶךְ king ➢ מֶ֫לֶךְ king of

2. **Vowel Reduction in Closed Syllables**. In the construct state, changeable long vowels in a closed syllable will reduce to a short vowel.

   מִשְׁפָּט judgment ➢ מִשְׁפַּט judgment of

   דָּבָר word ➢ דְּבַר word of

   בֵּן son ➢ בֶּן son of

   כֹּל all ➢ כָּל all of

3. **Vowel Reduction in Open Syllables**. In the construct state, changeable long vowels in an open syllable will reduce to Vocal Shewa (or Hateph Pathach with gutturals).

נָבִיא prophet	➢	נְבִיא prophet of
דָבָר word	➢	דְבַר word of
הָמוֹן multitude	➢	הֲמוֹן multitude of

4. **Masculine Plural Nouns**. The masculine plural ending ִים (and the dual ending ַ֫יִם) changes to ֵי (Tsere Yod) in the construct state.

אֱלֹהִים God	➢	אֱלֹהֵי God of
בָּנִים sons	➢	בְּנֵי sons of
עֵינַ֫יִם two eyes	➢	עֵינֵי (two) eyes of

5. **Feminine Singular Nouns**. The feminine singular ending ָה (Qamets He) changes to ַת (Pathach Taw) in the construct state.

תּוֹרָה law	➢	תּוֹרַת law of
מַלְכָּה queen	➢	מַלְכַּת queen of
שָׁנָה year	➢	שְׁנַת year of

6. **Plural Segholate Nouns**. In the construct state, plural Segholate nouns begin with a short vowel in a closed syllable.

עֶ֫בֶד servant	➢	עַבְדֵי servants of
שֵׁ֫בֶט tribe	➢	שִׁבְטֵי tribes of
חֹ֫דֶשׁ month	➢	חָדְשֵׁי months of

7. **Monosyllabic Nouns**. Certain (not all!) singular monosyllabic nouns add Hireq Yod to their stem in the construct state. This also occurs when these same nouns take pronominal suffixes. Be careful not to confuse this Hireq Yod with the 1cs pronominal suffix.

אָב father	➢	אֲבִי father of
		אָבִי my father
אָח brother	➢	אֲחִי brother of
		אָחִי my brother

Note that the above construct nouns have a reduced vowel, Hateph Pathach, under the first root letter. The nouns with a pronominal suffix maintain the long vowel, Qamets, under the first root letter.

8. **Diphthongs**. In the construct state, the AY diphthong (e.g., בַּ֫יִת) changes to Tsere Yod and the AW diphthong (e.g., מָ֫וֶת) changes to Holem Waw.

בַּ֫יִת house	➢	בֵּית house of
מָ֫וֶת death	➢	מוֹת death of

9. **Nouns Ending with Seghol He**. Nouns ending with Seghol He (e.g., שָׂדֶה) are masculine. In the singular construct, Seghol He changes to Tsere He.

שָׂדֶה field	➢	שְׂדֵה field of
מַחֲנֶה camp	➢	מַחֲנֵה camp of

10. **Tsere Changes to Pathach**. In certain words, Tsere changes to Pathach in a final closed syllable.

מִזְבֵּחַ altar	➢	מִזְבַּח altar of
זָקֵן elder	➢	זְקַן elder of

11. **First Rule of Shewa**. In plural nouns like בְּרָכוֹת and דְּבָרִים, the Qamets under the second root letter reduces to Vocal Shewa in the construct state and then the First Rule of Shewa applies.

בְּרָכוֹת blessings	➢	בִּרְכוֹת blessings of
דְּבָרִים words	➢	דִּבְרֵי words of

In the first example above, the Qamets under ר in בְּרָכוֹת changes to Shewa (בְּרְכוֹת) in the construct state. Two initial, side-by-side Vocal Shewas are not permitted and so the First Rule of Shewa is applied, producing בִּרְכוֹת. The same changes are also exhibited in the second example.

NUMBERS

Biblical Hebrew does not have a separate set of numerical symbols (1, 2, 3, etc.). Hebrew numbers are written out (one, two, three, etc.). There are both cardinal and ordinal numbers. Cardinal numbers are used for counting (one, two, three, etc.) and ordinal numbers are used to indicate position in a series (first, second, third, etc.).

One through Ten

	Masculine Absolute	Masculine Construct	Feminine Absolute	Feminine Construct
One	אֶחָד	אַחַד	אַחַת	אַחַת
Two	שְׁנַיִם	שְׁנֵי	שְׁתַּיִם	שְׁתֵּי
Three	שָׁלֹשׁ	שְׁלֹשׁ	שְׁלֹשָׁה	שְׁלֹשֶׁת
Four	אַרְבַּע	אַרְבַּע	אַרְבָּעָה	אַרְבַּעַת
Five	חָמֵשׁ	חֲמֵשׁ	חֲמִשָּׁה	חֲמֵשֶׁת
Six	שֵׁשׁ	שֵׁשׁ	שִׁשָּׁה	שֵׁשֶׁת
Seven	שֶׁבַע	שְׁבַע	שִׁבְעָה	שִׁבְעַת
Eight	שְׁמֹנֶה	שְׁמֹנֶה	שְׁמֹנָה	שְׁמֹנַת
Nine	תֵּשַׁע	תְּשַׁע	תִּשְׁעָה	תִּשְׁעַת
Ten	עֶשֶׂר	עֶשֶׂר	עֲשָׂרָה	עֲשֶׂרֶת

Notes: One through Ten

1. The number **one** is used like an **adjective**. It will follow the noun it modifies and agree in gender and definiteness. When used in the construct state, it will precede an absolute noun that is usually plural.

2. Number **two** is dual in number and classified as a **noun**. It agrees in gender with the other noun to which it is related. The absolute and construct forms are used interchangeably without any apparent change in meaning.

3. With numbers **three through ten**, there is no change in spelling, except to indicate gender and state. These numbers are classified as **nouns**, but they do not agree in gender with the other nouns to which they are related. In other words, masculine numbers can be used with feminine nouns and feminine numbers can be used with masculine nouns. Note also that while the numbers are singular in form, the nouns are plural. This phenomenon is often called **chiastic concord**.

Eleven through Nineteen

	with Masculine Nouns	with Feminine Nouns
Eleven	אַחַד עָשָׂר	אַחַת עֶשְׂרֵה
	עַשְׁתֵּי עָשָׂר	עַשְׁתֵּי עֶשְׂרֵה
Twelve	שְׁנֵי עָשָׂר	שְׁתֵּי עֶשְׂרֵה
	שְׁנֵים עָשָׂר	שְׁתֵּים עֶשְׂרֵה
Thirteen	שְׁלֹשָׁה עָשָׂר	שְׁלֹשׁ עֶשְׂרֵה
Fourteen	אַרְבָּעָה עָשָׂר	אַרְבַּע עֶשְׂרֵה
Fifteen	חֲמִשָּׁה עָשָׂר	חֲמֵשׁ עֶשְׂרֵה
Sixteen	שִׁשָּׁה עָשָׂר	שֵׁשׁ עֶשְׂרֵה
Seventeen	שִׁבְעָה עָשָׂר	שְׁבַע עֶשְׂרֵה
Eighteen	שְׁמֹנָה עָשָׂר	שְׁמֹנֶה עֶשְׂרֵה
Nineteen	תִּשְׁעָה עָשָׂר	תְּשַׁע עֶשְׂרֵה

Notes: Eleven through Nineteen

1. Note that eleven and twelve have alternate forms. The alternate form for eleven (with עַשְׁתֵּי) occurs only nineteen times in the Hebrew Bible.

2. Most of the time, these numbers occur with plural nouns. A few nouns, however, appear regularly in the singular. When singular nouns of this type occur with these numbers, they are translated as plural nouns.

Twenty through Ninety Nine

Twenty	עֶשְׂרִים
Thirty	שְׁלֹשִׁים
Forty	אַרְבָּעִים
Fifty	חֲמִשִּׁים
Sixty	שִׁשִּׁים
Seventy	שִׁבְעִים
Eighty	שְׁמֹנִים
Ninety	תִּשְׁעִים

Notes: Twenty through Ninety Nine

1. The number twenty (עֶשְׂרִים) is the masculine plural form of ten (עֶשֶׂר). Numbers thirty through ninety (by ten) are the masculine plural forms of three through nine.

2. In Hebrew, twenty-one and other such numbers occur either as "twenty and one" or, less frequently, as "one and twenty."

עֶשְׂרִים וְאַחַת	twenty-one
שִׁבְעִים וְשִׁבְעָה	seventy-seven
תִּשְׁעִים וָתֵשַׁע	ninety-nine
שְׁנַיִם וּשְׁלֹשִׁים	thirty-two

One Hundred and Up

One Hundred	מֵאָה
Two Hundred	מָאתַ֫יִם
Three Hundred	שְׁלֹשׁ מֵאוֹת
One Thousand	אֶ֫לֶף
Two Thousand	אַלְפַּ֫יִם
Three Thousand	שְׁלֹ֫שֶׁת אֲלָפִים
Ten Thousand	רְבָבָה
Twenty Thousand	רִבּוֹתַ֫יִם
Thirty Thousand	שְׁלֹשׁ רִבּוֹת

Notes: One Hundred and Up

1. Note that two hundred (מָאתַ֫יִם) is the dual form of one hundred (מֵאָה), two thousand (אַלְפַּ֫יִם) is the dual form of one thousand (אֶ֫לֶף), and twenty thousand (רִבּוֹתַ֫יִם) is the dual form of ten thousand (רְבָבָה).

2. The remaining numerical sequences (three hundred, four hundred, five hundred, six hundred, etc.) follow the pattern exhibited by three hundred (שְׁלֹשׁ מֵאוֹת), three thousand (שְׁלֹ֫שֶׁת אֲלָפִים), and thirty thousand (שְׁלֹשׁ רִבּוֹת).

Ordinal Numbers	Masculine	Feminine
First	רִאשׁוֹן	רִאשׁוֹנָה
Second	שֵׁנִי	שֵׁנִית
Third	שְׁלִישִׁי	שְׁלִישִׁית
Fourth	רְבִיעִי	רְבִיעִית
Fifth	חֲמִישִׁי	חֲמִישִׁית
Sixth	שִׁשִּׁי	שִׁשִּׁית
Seventh	שְׁבִיעִי	שְׁבִיעִית
Eighth	שְׁמִינִי	שְׁמִינִית
Ninth	תְּשִׁיעִי	תְּשִׁיעִית
Tenth	עֲשִׂירִי	עֲשִׂירִית

Notes: Ordinal Numbers

1. The ordinal רִאשׁוֹן (first) is derived from the noun רֹאשׁ (head, chief, beginning). The remaining ordinals share a common root with their corresponding cardinal number. For example, שֵׁשׁ (six) and שִׁשִּׁי (sixth) share a common root.

2. With ordinals second through tenth, the masculine forms end with Hireq Yod, as in שְׁלִישִׁי, and feminine forms end with Taw, as in שְׁלִישִׁית.

3. Ordinal numbers are adjectives. When attributive, they follow the noun and usually agree in gender and definiteness.

בַּיּוֹם הָרִאשׁוֹן	on the first day
בַּיּוֹם הַשְּׁבִיעִי	on the seventh day
יוֹם הַשִּׁשִּׁי	the sixth day

4. For ordinals greater than tenth, cardinal numbers are used.

וּשְׁלֹשׁ־עֶשְׂרֵה שָׁנָה	and the thirteenth year
בִּשְׁלֹשִׁים וָשֶׁבַע שָׁנָה	in the thirty-seventh year
בִּשְׁנַת הָאַרְבָּעִים	in the fortieth year

PARTICLES

Interrogative Particle הֲ

In addition to interrogative pronouns, Hebrew also has an interrogative particle. In Hebrew, questions are not created with punctuation as in English (?). Rather, interrogative clauses (those that ask a question) are created either with the use of certain interrogative pronouns or with a form of the particle הֲ prefixed to the first word of the sentence.

הֲשֹׁמֵר אָחִי אָנֹכִי

Am I the keeper of my brother?

הֲמָלֹךְ תִּמְלֹךְ עָלֵינוּ

Will you indeed rule over us?

In both examples above, the sentences begin with the interrogative particle הֲ prefixed to the first word of the clause. In each case, the question has been created by the prefixing of this interrogative particle.

The spelling of the particle will change, depending on the spelling of the form to which it is prefixed.

1. Prefixed to most consonants, the interrogative particle is spelled הֲ.
2. Prefixed to a guttural consonant or any consonant with Shewa, it is spelled הַ.
3. Prefixed to a guttural consonant followed by Qamets, the spelling of the particle is הֶ.

Directional Particle ָה

In Hebrew, a special ending may be added to a word in order to express the idea of motion toward someone or something. This ending is the directional particle ָה (Qamets He). It is always unaccented. In terms of meaning, the use of the directional ending is the same as a prepositional phrase with אֶל (to, toward).

בַּ֫יִת	הַבַּ֫יְתָה	to (toward) the house
עִיר	הָעִ֫ירָה	to (toward) the city
שָׁמַ֫יִם	הַשָּׁמַ֫יְמָה	to heaven, heavenward
מִצְרַ֫יִם	מִצְרַ֫יְמָה	to (toward) Egypt
הַר	הָהָ֫רָה	to (toward) the mountain
שָׁם	שָׁ֫מָּה	to there, to that place
יָם	יָ֫מָּה	toward the sea, westward

Particle הִנֵּה

The particle הִנֵּה (also הֵן and הֶן־) is commonly translated "behold." This particle could be called a *demonstrative interjection*, but this is only one of its many uses. It can stand alone or take Type 1 pronominal suffixes. The attested forms are presented below.

3ms	הִנּוֹ	3mp	הִנָּם
2ms	הִנְּךָ	2mp	הִנְּכֶם
2fs	הִנָּךְ	2fp	
1cs	הִנֵּ֫נִי/הִנְנִי	1cp	הִנֶּ֫נּוּ/הִנְנוּ

The particle הִנֵּה is used in a number of different ways, but three common uses are detailed below.

1. The particle הִנֵּה may be used to highlight or stress the importance of something (demonstrative interjection).

וַיַּרְא אֱלֹהִים אֶת־כָּל־אֲשֶׁר עָשָׂה וְהִנֵּה־טוֹב מְאֹד
And God saw all that he had made, and *behold* (right then), (it was) very good.

הִנֵּה עֵין יְהוָה אֶל־יְרֵאָיו
Behold, the eye of Yahweh is upon those who fear him.

2. The particle הִנֵּה may be used to indicate the immediate presence of someone or something with an emphasis on immediacy and urgency.

וְהִנֵּה אָנֹכִי עִמָּךְ
And *behold,* I am with you (at this very moment).

וַיֹּאמֶר הִנֵּנִי
And he said, "I am (right) *here*."

3. The particle הִנֵּה may be used to introduce a fact or situation upon which a subsequent statement is based.

וַיֹּאמֶר שְׁמוּאֵל אֶל־כָּל־יִשְׂרָאֵל
הִנֵּה שָׁמַעְתִּי בְקֹלְכֶם לְכֹל אֲשֶׁר־אֲמַרְתֶּם לִי
וָאַמְלִיךְ עֲלֵיכֶם מֶלֶךְ

And Samuel said to all of Israel,
"*Behold,* I have listened to all that you have said to me
and I have caused a king to reign over you."

הִנֵּה־נָא יָדַעְתִּי כִּי אִשָּׁה יְפַת־מַרְאֶה אָתְּ
וְהָיָה כִּי־יִרְאוּ אֹתָךְ הַמִּצְרִים
וְהָרְגוּ אֹתִי וְאֹתָךְ יְחַיּוּ

Behold, I know that you are a woman with a beautiful
appearance and when the Egyptians see you
they will kill me but let you live.

The Particle of Existence יֵשׁ

Hebrew may express the *existence* of someone or something by using the particle יֵשׁ (also spelled יֶשׁ־), which translates either "(there) is" or "(there) are." This particle does not change its spelling to indicate gender or number.

אָכֵן יֵשׁ יְהוָה בַּמָּקוֹם הַזֶּה
Surely Yahweh *is* in this place.

יֵשׁ־אֱלֹהִים שֹׁפְטִים בָּאָרֶץ
There is a God who judges on the earth.

The particle יֵשׁ may also be used to express possession when followed by the preposition לְ (to).

יֶשׁ־לִי תִקְוָה
I have hope (lit. *There is* to me hope).

הֲיֵשׁ לָכֶם אָח
Do you have a brother (lit. *Is there* to you a brother)?

The Particle of Nonexistence אַ֫יִן

Hebrew may express the *nonexistence* or absence of someone or something by using the particle אַ֫יִן (spelled אֵין in construct), which translates either "(there) is not" or "(there) are not." This particle is not inflected for person, gender, or number.

אֵין־יוֹסֵף בַּבּוֹר
Joseph *was not* in the cistern.

וְאֵין־דַּעַת אֱלֹהִים בָּאָרֶץ
And *there is no* knowledge of God in the land.

The particle אֵין may also be used to express *lack of possession* when followed by the preposition לְ (to).

אֵין לוֹ בֵּן
He had no son (lit. *there was not* to him a son).

אֵין־לָנוּ חֵלֶק בְּדָוִד
We have no portion in David
(lit. *There is not* to us a portion in David)

The particle אֵין may appear with pronominal suffixes or it may be used to negate a verbless clause.

אֵינָם יְרֵאִים אֶת־יְהוָה
They do not fear Yahweh.

אָמַר נָבָל בְּלִבּוֹ אֵין אֱלֹהִים
A fool says in his heart, God *does not exist*.

VERBLESS CLAUSES

Introduction

A clause contains a subject and a predicate. The subject is what the clause is about (topic), and the predicate provides information about the subject (comment). Hebrew is also capable of indicating predication without an explicit verb, with the so-called *verbless* clause.

Verbless Clause Components

A verbless clause consists of a subject and a noun or its equivalent serving as the predicate. The subject and the predicate appear together (side by side), and they may consist of a noun, adjective, independent personal pronoun, demonstrative pronoun, interrogative pronoun, prepositional phrase, or participle as the following examples illustrate. In English, a form of the verb "to be" is used to translate the predication.

גָּדוֹל כְּבוֹדוֹ

His glory *is* great.

מִי־הָאִישׁ הֶחָכָם

Who *is* the wise man?

זֹאת הַבְּרִית

This *is* the covenant.

וְחֹשֶׁךְ עַל־פְּנֵי תְהוֹם

And darkness *was* over the face of the deep.

Word Order and Types of Verbless Clauses

In Hebrew, the word order for a verbless clause is variable, but this variation is often meaningful. If the word order is *subject-predicate*, it may be understood as a verbless clause of *identification* in order to indicate "who" or "what" is the subject. If the word order is *predicate-subject*, it may be understood as a verbless clause of *classification* in order to indicate the general class to which the subject belongs. In the following examples, the subjects appear in red.

אָנֹכִי מָגֵן לָךְ

I *am* your shield (identification).

עָפָר אַתָּה

You *are* dust (classification).

Verbless Clauses with a Third Person Pronoun

A third person independent personal pronoun may appear in a verbless clause an as indicator of predication. In this usage, the pronoun is not translated.

וַיהוָה הוּא הַהֹלֵךְ לְפָנֶיךָ

Yahweh *is* the one who goes before you.

יִרְאַת יְהוָה הִיא אוֹצָרוֹ

The fear of Yahweh *is* his treasure.

אַתָּה־הוּא מַלְכִּי אֱלֹהִים

You *are* my king, O God.

QAL PERFECT

Qal Perfect Paradigm: Strong Verbs

	Sufformative	Perfect	Translation
3ms		קָטַל	he killed
3fs	ָה	קָֽטְלָה	she killed
2ms	תָּ	קָטַ֫לְתָּ	you killed
2fs	תְּ	קָטַלְתְּ	you killed
1cs	תִּי	קָטַ֫לְתִּי	I killed
3cp	וּ	קָֽטְלוּ	they killed
2mp	תֶּם	קְטַלְתֶּם	you killed
2fp	תֶּן	קְטַלְתֶּן	you killed
1cp	נוּ	קָטַ֫לְנוּ	we killed

Notes: Strong Verbs

1. In the Perfect (or "suffix") conjugation, a sufformative appears at the end of each verb, except the 3ms, marking the verb's person, gender, and number.

2. Three forms of the Perfect conjugation are listed as common, meaning not inflected for gender. The common forms are 1cs (קָטַ֫לְתִּי), 1cp (קָטַ֫לְנוּ), and 3cp (קָֽטְלוּ). These verbs may be used with either masculine or feminine subjects.

3. Note the presence of the Metheg in the 3fs (קָֽטְלָה) and 3cp (קָֽטְלוּ) forms. The Metheg identifies the vowel as Qamets and not Qamets Hatuf.

4. Note the presence of the accent mark (on the penultima syllable) in the 2ms (קָטַ֫לְתָּ), 1cs (קָטַ֫לְתִּי), and 1cp (קָטַ֫לְנוּ) forms.

Qal Perfect Paradigms: Stative Verbs

	Pathach Stative	Tsere Stative	Holem Stative	Strong Verb
3ms	גָּדַל	כָּבֵד	קָטֹן	קָטַל
3fs	גָּֽדְלָה	כָּֽבְדָה	קָֽטְנָה	קָֽטְלָה
2ms	גָּדַ֫לְתָּ	כָּבַ֫דְתָּ	קָטֹ֫נְתָּ	קָטַ֫לְתָּ
2fs	גָּדַלְתְּ	כָּבַדְתְּ	קָטֹנְתְּ	קָטַלְתְּ
1cs	גָּדַ֫לְתִּי	כָּבַ֫דְתִּי	קָטֹ֫נְתִּי	קָטַ֫לְתִּי
3cp	גָּֽדְלוּ	כָּֽבְדוּ	קָֽטְנוּ	קָֽטְלוּ
2mp	גְּדַלְתֶּם	כְּבַדְתֶּם	קְטָנְתֶּם	קְטַלְתֶּם
2fp	גְּדַלְתֶּן	כְּבַדְתֶּן	קְטָנְתֶּן	קְטַלְתֶּן
1cp	גָּדַ֫לְנוּ	כָּבַ֫דְנוּ	קָטֹ֫נּוּ	קָטַ֫לְנוּ

Notes: Stative Verbs

1. Stative verbs describe the state or condition of the subject (he is old, she is wise) rather than describing a verbal action (he wrote, she observed).

2. Stative verbs are classified by their stem vowel: Pathach stative (גָּדַל), Tsere Stative (כָּבֵד), and Holem stative (קָטֹן).
3. The Pathach-Stative (גָּדַל) is spelled just like the regular strong verb.
4. With the Tsere-Stative, the Tsere stem vowel appears only in the 3ms form (כָּבֵד). All other forms are spelled just like the regular strong verb.
5. With the Holem-Stative, an o-class stem vowel appears throughout the paradigm (except in the 3fs and 3cp). Note the o-class vowel Qamets Hatuf in the 2mp (קְטָנְתֶּם) and 2fp (קְטָנְתֶּן) forms.

Qal Perfect Paradigms: Weak Verbs 1

	I-Guttural	II-Guttural	III-ח/ע	III-א
3ms	עָמַד	בָּחַר	שָׁמַע	מָצָא
3fs	עָֽמְדָה	בָּֽחֲרָה	שָֽׁמְעָה	מָֽצְאָה
2ms	עָמַדְתָּ	בָּחַרְתָּ	שָׁמַעְתָּ	מָצָאתָ
2fs	עָמַדְתְּ	בָּחַרְתְּ	שָׁמַעַתְּ	מָצָאת
1cs	עָמַדְתִּי	בָּחַרְתִּי	שָׁמַעְתִּי	מָצָאתִי
3cp	עָֽמְדוּ	בָּֽחֲרוּ	שָֽׁמְעוּ	מָֽצְאוּ
2mp	עֲמַדְתֶּם	בְּחַרְתֶּם	שְׁמַעְתֶּם	מְצָאתֶם
2fp	עֲמַדְתֶּן	בְּחַרְתֶּן	שְׁמַעְתֶּן	מְצָאתֶן
1cp	עָמַדְנוּ	בָּחַרְנוּ	שָׁמַעְנוּ	מָצָאנוּ

Notes: Weak Verbs 1

1. With I-Guttural and II-Guttural verbs, Vocal Shewa changes to Hateph Pathach under the guttural consonants.
2. With III-ח/ע verbs, the Silent Shewa in the 2fs form changes to Pathach (שָׁמַ֫עַתְּ).
3. With III-א verbs, the א is quiescent and the stem vowel lengthens to Qamets. As a result, the Daghesh Lene in the ת of the Perfect sufformative drops out. The changes in the 2fs (מָצָאת) should be carefully noted.

Qal Perfect Paradigms: Weak Verbs 2

	III-ה	Biconsonantal	Geminate	I-Gutt/III-ה
3ms	בָּנָה	קָם	סָבַב	עָלָה
3fs	בָּֽנְתָה	קָ֫מָה	סָֽבְבָה	עָֽלְתָה
2ms	בָּנִ֫יתָ	קַ֫מְתָּ	סַבּ֫וֹתָ	עָלִ֫יתָ
2fs	בָּנִית	קַמְתְּ	סַבּוֹת	עָלִית
1cs	בָּנִ֫יתִי	קַ֫מְתִּי	סַבּ֫וֹתִי	עָלִ֫יתִי
3cp	בָּנוּ	קָ֫מוּ	סָֽבְבוּ	עָלוּ
2mp	בְּנִיתֶם	קַמְתֶּם	סַבּוֹתֶם	עֲלִיתֶם
2fp	בְּנִיתֶן	קַמְתֶּן	סַבּוֹתֶן	עֲלִיתֶן
1cp	בָּנִ֫ינוּ	קַ֫מְנוּ	סַבּ֫וֹנוּ	עָלִ֫ינוּ

Notes: Weak Verbs 2

1. Most III-ה verbs were originally III-י (Yod). This original Yod "reappears" as Hireq Yod in the first and second persons (e.g. בָּנִ֫יתָ). Note that the presence of the Hireq Yod causes the Daghesh Lene in the ת of the Perfect sufformatives to drop out. In the 3fs form (בָּֽנְתָה), ה becomes ת before the Perfect sufformative.

2. With Biconsonantal verbs, all third person forms have Qamets under the first root consonant (e.g., קָ֫מָה), and all second and first person forms have Pathach (e.g., קַ֫מְתָּ).

3. With Geminate verbs, third person forms follow the strong verb pattern. The second and first person forms are identified by a Daghesh Forte in the remaining Geminate consonant and a Holem Waw connecting vowel before the Perfect sufformative (e.g., סַבּ֫וֹתָ). Note that the presence of the Holem Waw causes the Daghesh Lene in the ת of the Perfect sufformatives to drop out.

Syntax of the Perfect Conjugation

1. **Regular Perfect**. When used to describe a completed action, the Hebrew Perfect may be translated by the English past tense (he studied), present perfect (he has studied), past perfect (he had studied), or future perfect (he will have studied). When used to describe a state of being, it will be translated with the English present tense (he is wise) or past tense (he was wise). The

Hebrew Perfect may also be translated by the English present tense with verbs of perception or attitude (he knows, he loves). When a Perfect verb is used to describe a completed action, it is normally *not* the first word in its clause, though there are exceptions.

בַּיּוֹם הַהוּא כָּרַת יְהוָה אֶת־אַבְרָם בְּרִית

In that day, Yahweh *made (cut)* a covenant with Abram.

בְּרֵאשִׁית בָּרָא אֱלֹהִים אֵת הַשָּׁמַיִם וְאֵת הָאָרֶץ

In the beginning, God *created* the heavens and the earth.

2. **Consecutive Perfect**. When a Perfect verb is prefixed with the Waw Consecutive, it will be translated with the values of the Imperfect. The Waw Consecutive with the Perfect is spelled just like the regular conjunction (וְקָטַל). The consecutive Perfect is commonly used for future tense narrative sequences (and also to express habitual-durative action) and appears as the first word in its clause.

וְאָהַבְתָּ אֵת יְהוָה אֱלֹהֶיךָ

And *you will love* Yahweh your God.

וְזָכַרְתִּי אֶת־בְּרִיתִי

And *I will remember* my covenant.

3. **Regular Perfect with Conjunction** וְ. The Perfect may appear with the regular conjunction וְ and *not* the Waw Consecutive. In these instances, the verbal construction is translated with "and" plus

the past (or present) tense of the verb, as in וְקָטַל (and he killed). There are two basic contexts in which the Perfect with the regular conjunction וְ may appear.

First, the Perfect with the regular conjunction וְ may occur in a short series of Perfect verbs. In this context, the first verb in the series will be the regular Perfect. The Perfect verbs that follow may be joined by the regular conjunction וְ and should be translated with the temporal value of the first Perfect verb.

וַאֲנִי זָקַנְתִּי וָשַׂבְתִּי

But as for me, *I am old and I am gray*.

אָבִיךָ הֲלוֹא אָכַל וְשָׁתָה וְעָשָׂה מִשְׁפָּט

As for your father, did he not *eat and drink and do justice*?

Second, the Perfect with the regular conjunction וְ may occur in a series of short (syntactically) parallel clauses. In this context, both clauses contain a Perfect verb, the second of which is prefixed with the regular conjunction וְ and not the Waw Consecutive.

הִנֵּה נָגַע זֶה עַל־שְׂפָתֶיךָ וְסָר עֲוֹנֶךָ

Behold, *he touched* this upon your lips *and he removed* your iniquity.

כִּי־פָדָה יְהוָה אֶת־יַעֲקֹב וּגְאָלוֹ מִיַּד חָזָק מִמֶּנּוּ

For Yahweh *ransomed* Jacob and *he redeemed* him from the hand of one stronger than he.

4. **Imperative-Consecutive Perfect Sequence.** An Imperative may be followed by a consecutive Perfect. In this sequence, the Perfect verb may carry the full force of the preceding Imperative in its translation.

לֵךְ וְאָמַרְתָּ אֶל־עַבְדִּי

Go *and say* to my servant.

וַיֹּאמֶר צֵא וְעָמַדְתָּ בָהָר לִפְנֵי יְהוָה

And he said, "Go out *and stand* on the mountain before Yahweh."

QAL IMPERFECT

Qal Imperfect Paradigm: Strong Verbs

	Suffor-mative	Imperfect	Prefor-mative	Translation
3ms		יִקְטֹל	יִ	he will kill
3fs		תִּקְטֹל	תִּ	she will kill
2ms		תִּקְטֹל	תִּ	you will kill
2fs	ִי	תִּקְטְלִי	תִּ	you will kill
1cs		אֶקְטֹל	אֶ	I will kill
3mp	וּ	יִקְטְלוּ	יִ	they will kill
3fp	נָה	תִּקְטֹלְנָה	תִּ	they will kill
2mp	וּ	תִּקְטְלוּ	תִּ	you will kill
2fp	נָה	תִּקְטֹלְנָה	תִּ	you will kill
1cp		נִקְטֹל	נִ	we will kill

Notes: Strong Verbs

1. In the Imperfect (or "prefix") conjugation, a verbal preformative appears at the beginning of each verb. Additionally, five forms appear with a sufformative (2fs, 3mp, 3fp, 2mp, 2fp). The Imperfect preformatives and sufformatives mark the verb's person, gender, and number.

2. In the Qal strong verb, the preformative consonant is Hireq, except in the 1cs form, which has Seghol (אֶקְטֹל).

3. Two sets of forms are identical in the Imperfect conjugation, the 3fs/2ms (תִּקְטֹל) and the 3fp/2fp (תִּקְטֹלְנָה).

4. In the Perfect, the third person plural form קָטְלוּ (they killed) is common in gender. In the Imperfect, the third person plural is inflected for gender and so there are two third person plural forms, the 3mp יִקְטְלוּ and the 3fp תִּקְטֹלְנָה.

5. The 3mp and the 2mp forms may be written with a final ן as in יִקְטְלוּן or תִּקְטְלוּן. This final ן is called *Nun Paragogicum*. Verbs with this final Nun may also be spelled defectively, as in יִקְטְלֻן or תִּקְטְלֻן (with Qibbuts instead of Shureq).

Negation of the Imperfect

Imperfect verbs can be negated with one of two negative particles, לֹא and אַל. The negative particle לֹא is more common and may be used before an Imperfect verb to express an *absolute or permanent* prohibition. The negative particle אַל is less common and is used to express an *immediate and specific* prohibition.

לֹא תִּנְאָף

You shall *not* commit adultery.

אַל־תִּירָא

Do *not* fear!

Qal Imperfect Paradigms: Stative Verbs

	Pathach Stative	Tsere Stative	Holem Stative	Strong Verb
3ms	יִגְדַּל	יִכְבַּד	יִקְטַן	יִקְטֹל
3fs	תִּגְדַּל	תִּכְבַּד	תִּקְטַן	תִּקְטֹל
2ms	תִּגְדַּל	תִּכְבַּד	תִּקְטַן	תִּקְטֹל
2fs	תִּגְדְּלִי	תִּכְבְּדִי	תִּקְטְנִי	תִּקְטְלִי
1cs	אֶגְדַּל	אֶכְבַּד	אֶקְטַן	אֶקְטֹל
3mp	יִגְדְּלוּ	יִכְבְּדוּ	יִקְטְנוּ	יִקְטְלוּ
3fp	תִּגְדַּלְנָה	תִּכְבַּדְנָה	תִּקְטַנָּה	תִּקְטֹלְנָה
2mp	תִּגְדְּלוּ	תִּכְבְּדוּ	תִּקְטְנוּ	תִּקְטְלוּ
2fp	תִּגְדַּלְנָה	תִּכְבַּדְנָה	תִּקְטַנָּה	תִּקְטֹלְנָה
1cp	נִגְדַּל	נִכְבַּד	נִקְטַן	נִקְטֹל

Notes: Stative Verbs

1. Stative verbs are classified by their stem vowel in the Perfect: Pathach (גָּדַל), Tsere (כָּבֵד), or Holem (קָטֹן).

2. With the Imperfect stative verb, the stem vowel is Pathach throughout, regardless of the original stem vowel in the Perfect. Note that the Pathach stem vowel of the Imperfect stative is distinct from the Holem stem vowel of the regular Imperfect strong verb form (יִקְטֹל).

Qal Imperfect Paradigms: Weak Verbs 1

	II-Guttural	III-ע/ח	III-א
3ms	יִבְחַר	יִשְׁלַח	יִמְצָא
3fs	תִּבְחַר	תִּשְׁלַח	תִּמְצָא
2ms	תִּבְחַר	תִּשְׁלַח	תִּמְצָא
2fs	תִּבְחֲרִי	תִּשְׁלְחִי	תִּמְצְאִי
1cs	אֶבְחַר	אֶשְׁלַח	אֶמְצָא
3mp	יִבְחֲרוּ	יִשְׁלְחוּ	יִמְצְאוּ
3fp	תִּבְחַ֫רְנָה	תִּשְׁלַ֫חְנָה	תִּמְצֶ֫אנָה
2mp	תִּבְחֲרוּ	תִּשְׁלְחוּ	תִּמְצְאוּ
2fp	תִּבְחַ֫רְנָה	תִּשְׁלַ֫חְנָה	תִּמְצֶ֫אנָה
1cp	נִבְחַר	נִשְׁלַח	נִמְצָא

Notes: Weak Verbs 1

1. With II-Guttural and III-ע/ח verbs, the stem vowel is Pathach instead of Holem. Additionally, in II-Guttural verbs, Hateph Pathach appears in the place of Vocal Shewa.

2. With III-**א** verbs, the **א** is quiescent and the stem vowel lengthens to Qamets (just like the Perfect). Additionally, The twin 3fp and 2fp forms (תִּמְצֶ֫אנָה) exhibit an unexpected Seghol stem vowel.

Qal Imperfect Paradigms: Weak Verbs 2

	I-Guttural Type 1	I-Guttural Type 2	I-Guttural Type 3
3ms	יֶחֱזַק	יַעֲמֹד	יֹאמַר
3fs	תֶּחֱזַק	תַּעֲמֹד	תֹּאמַר
2ms	תֶּחֱזַק	תַּעֲמֹד	תֹּאמַר
2fs	תֶּחֶזְקִי	תַּעַמְדִי	תֹּאמְרִי
1cs	אֶחֱזַק	אֶעֱמֹד	אֹמַר
3mp	יֶחֶזְקוּ	יַעַמְדוּ	יֹאמְרוּ
3fp	תֶּחֱזַ֫קְנָה	תַּעֲמֹ֫דְנָה	תֹּאמַ֫רְנָה
2mp	תֶּחֶזְקוּ	תַּעַמְדוּ	תֹּאמְרוּ
2fp	תֶּחֱזַ֫קְנָה	תַּעֲמֹ֫דְנָה	תֹּאמַ֫רְנָה
1cp	נֶחֱזַק	נַעֲמֹד	נֹאמַר

Notes: Weak Verbs 2

1. Type 1 verbs with the **Pathach stem vowel** exhibit a Seghol preformative vowel followed by a Hateph Seghol under the guttural in first root position (יֶחֱזַק). With those forms having a sufformative consisting of a vowel (2fs, 3mp, 2mp), the vowel under the guttural is Seghol in a closed syllable (תֶּחֶזְקוּ).

2. Type 2 verbs with the **Holem stem vowel** generally exhibit a Pathach preformative vowel and a

Hateph Pathach under the guttural in first root position (יַעֲמֹד). The only exception to this pattern is the 1cs form (אֶעֱמֹד). With those forms having a sufformative consisting of a vowel (2fs, 3mp, 2mp), the vowel under the guttural is Pathach in a closed syllable (תַּעַמְדִי).

3. There are six Type 3 I-Guttural verbs that begin with א: אָמַר (to say), אָכַל (to eat), אָבַד (to perish), אָחַז (to seize), אָפָה (to bake), and אָבָה (to be willing). The preformative vowel is Holem and the א is quiescent (יֹאמַר). Note also the 1cs form אֹמַר (I will say). The single א in this form represents both the א of the verbal root and the א of the 1cs preformative. Whether written once (אֹמַר) or twice (אֹאמַר), the pronunciation would be the same.

Qal Imperfect Paradigms: Weak Verbs 3

Biconsonantal verbs are composed of two rather than three root consonants. With the Imperfect and related conjugations, a medial vowel letter is found in every form. This medial vowel letter is used to classify the different types of biconsonantal verbs.

	Perfect 3ms	Imperfect 3ms	Infinitive Construct	
Shureq	קָם	יָקוּם	קוּם	to arise
Hireq Yod	שָׂם	יָשִׂים	שִׂים	to place
Holem Waw	בָּא	יָבוֹא	בּוֹא	to enter

	Biconsonantal קוּם	Biconsonantal שִׂים	Biconsonantal בּוֹא
3ms	יָקוּם	יָשִׂים	יָבוֹא
3fs	תָּקוּם	תָּשִׂים	תָּבוֹא
2ms	תָּקוּם	תָּשִׂים	תָּבוֹא
2fs	תָּקֽוּמִי	תָּשִׂ֫ימִי	תָּב֫וֹאִי
1cs	אָקוּם	אָשִׂים	אָבוֹא
3mp	יָק֫וּמוּ	יָשִׂ֫ימוּ	יָב֫וֹאוּ
3fp	תְּקוּמֶ֫ינָה	תְּשִׂימֶ֫ינָה	תָּב֫וֹאנָה
2mp	תָּק֫וּמוּ	תָּשִׂ֫ימוּ	תָּב֫וֹאוּ
2fp	תְּקוּמֶ֫ינָה	תְּשִׂימֶ֫ינָה	תָּב֫וֹאנָה
1cp	נָקוּם	נָשִׂים	נָבוֹא

Notes: Weak Verbs 3

1. In all forms (except 3fp and 2fp) and in every class, the preformative vowel is Qamets.
2. The stem vowel of every form is determined by the Biconsonantal sub-class: Shureq (יָקוּם), Hireq Yod (יָשִׂים), or Holem Waw (יָבוֹא).
3. It should be noted that some mixing of the stem vowel does occur. For example, יָשִׂים is sometimes rendered יָשׂוּם. Additionally, the stem vowel may be written defectively (e.g., יָקוּם may appear as יָקֻם).

Qal Imperfect Paradigms: Weak Verbs 4

	III-ה	I-י	I-נ	Geminate
3ms	יִבְנֶה	יֵשֵׁב	יִפֹּל	יָסֹב
3fs	תִּבְנֶה	תֵּשֵׁב	תִּפֹּל	תָּסֹב
2ms	תִּבְנֶה	תֵּשֵׁב	תִּפֹּל	תָּסֹב
2fs	תִּבְנִי	תֵּשְׁבִי	תִּפְּלִי	תָּסֹבִּי
1cs	אֶבְנֶה	אֵשֵׁב	אֶפֹּל	אָסֹב
3mp	יִבְנוּ	יֵשְׁבוּ	יִפְּלוּ	יָסֹבּוּ
3fp	תִּבְנֶינָה	תֵּשַׁבְנָה	תִּפֹּלְנָה	תְּסֻבֶּינָה
2mp	תִּבְנוּ	תֵּשְׁבוּ	תִּפְּלוּ	תָּסֹבּוּ
2fp	תִּבְנֶינָה	תֵּשַׁבְנָה	תִּפֹּלְנָה	תְּסֻבֶּינָה
1cp	נִבְנֶה	נֵשֵׁב	נִפֹּל	נָסֹב

Notes: Weak Verbs 4

1. The verbs in this grouping are triconsonantal (consisting of three root consonants), but only two root consonants appear in the Imperfect form. With weak verbs of this type, the verbal root must be reconstructed in order to correctly identify and translate the verbal construction.

2. With III-ה verbs, the five forms of the Imperfect without sufformatives end in Seghol He (יִבְנֶה). In the twin 3fp and 2fp forms, the Seghol Yod connecting vowel is distinctive. In the remaining

three forms, the absence of any other weak verb diagnostic indicators will be the key to identification as III-ה.

3. With I-י verbs (Type 1) and הָלַךְ, the first consonant of the verbal root has dropped out. This weak verb class is distinguished by the Tsere preformative vowel in each form (יֵשֵׁב).

4. With I-נ verbs and לָקַח, the first consonant of the verbal root has assimilated to the second consonant of the verbal root. The assimilated נ is represented as a Daghesh Forte in the second root consonant (יִפֹּל).

5. With Geminate verbs, only one Geminate consonant remains in the Imperfect conjugation. The five forms that take an Imperfect sufformative exhibit a Daghesh Forte in the remaining Geminate consonant (יָסֹ֫בּוּ). In those forms without the Daghesh Forte, you will want to use the same process of elimination as with III-ה verbs. Note, however, that Geminate verbs have a distinctive Qamets preformative vowel (יָסֹב).

Syntax of the Imperfect Conjugation

1. **Regular Imperfect**. The regular Imperfect is used to express incomplete action (whether in the past, present, or future) and is usually translated by the English future tense (I will study) or present tense (I study). When used in this way, the Imperfect verb does *not* normally appear as the first word in its clause.

הוּא יְשׁוּפְךָ רֹאשׁ וְאַתָּה תְּשׁוּפֶנּוּ עָקֵב

He will crush you on the head and
you will crush him on the heel.

יְהוָה יִמְלֹךְ לְעֹלָם וָעֶד

Yahweh *will reign* forever and ever.

2. **Consecutive Imperfect**. When an Imperfect verb is prefixed with the Waw Consecutive, it is normally translated as a simple past tense in English. The Waw Consecutive with the Imperfect is spelled as וַ with a Daghesh Forte in the Imperfect preformative (וַיִּקְטֹל). The consecutive Imperfect is commonly used for a past tense narrative sequence and appears as the first word in its clause.

וַיִּקַּח יְהוּדָה אִשָּׁה לְעֵר בְּכוֹרוֹ

And Judah *took* a wife for
Er, his firstborn.

וַתַּהַר לֵאָה וַתֵּלֶד בֵּן וַתִּקְרָא שְׁמוֹ רְאוּבֵן

And Leah *conceived and she bore* a son
and she called his name Reuben.

3. **Volitional Imperfect**. Also called Cohortative (first person) and Jussive (third person), the volitional Imperfect is normally the first word in its clause, though there are some exceptions.

יִשְׁפֹּט יְהוָה בֵּינִי וּבֵינֶיךָ

May Yahweh *judge* between me and you.

נַעֲשֶׂה אָדָם בְּצַלְמֵנוּ

Let us make man in our image.

4. **Imperative-Imperfect Sequence**. An Imperative verb may be followed by an Imperfect verb, a construction that will create a **purpose** or **result** clause. In this sequence, the Imperfect will be marked with the conjunction וְ (not Waw Consecutive) and may be translated as "so that."

רְדוּ־שָׁמָּה וְשִׁבְרוּ־לָנוּ מִשָּׁם וְנִחְיֶה

Go down there and buy grain for us from there *so that we might live.*

בֹּא הֵנָּה וְאֶשְׁלְחָה אֹתְךָ אֶל־הַמֶּלֶךְ

Come here *so that I may send* you to the king.

QAL IMPERATIVE

Qal Imperative Paradigm: Strong Verbs

	Sufformative	Imperative	Translation
2ms		קְטֹל	(you) kill!
2fs	ִי	קִטְלִי	(you) kill!
2mp	וּ	קִטְלוּ	(you) kill!
2fp	נָה	קְטֹלְנָה	(you) kill!

Notes: Strong Verbs

1. In general, the Imperative is used to express direct commands, demanding (immediate) action from the one being addressed. It can also be used to grant permission or to communicate a request.

2. The Hebrew Imperative occurs only in the second person, singular and plural. English translations do not normally use the second person pronoun (you) when rendering the Hebrew Imperative.

3. The forms of the Imperative are related to their corresponding Imperfect forms. Both the Imperative and the Imperfect (second person) share the same set of sufformatives. The Imperative verb does *not* take a preformative.

4. Imperative verbs are not negated. Negative commands are constructed with a negative particle (לֹא or אַל) and the Imperfect verb.

The Lengthened Imperative

The 2ms Imperative may appear with a Qamets He ending, as in קָטְלָה (kill!).[1] The vowel in the first syllable is Qamets Hatuf (קָטְלָה), not Qamets. The vowel under the first root letter may also be Hireq (e.g., שִׁמְעָה). The significance of this lengthened form is disputed (polite, emphatic, honorific, middle, etc.). It is normally translated just like the regular Imperative.

Lexical Form	Regular Imperative	Lengthened Imperative	Translation
שָׁמַר	שְׁמֹר	שָׁמְרָה	Keep!
שָׁמַע	שְׁמַע	שִׁמְעָה	Listen!
הָלַךְ	לֵךְ	לְכָה	Go!

The Particle נָא

The particle נָא may follow the Imperative verb. Frequently, it is joined to the Imperative by Maqqef. This particle is normally classified as an interjection and may indicate immediacy ("now"), politeness ("please"), or entreaty ("I wish"). It may also be left untranslated.

וַיֹּאמֶר אֲלֵיהֶם שִׁמְעוּ־נָא הַחֲלוֹם הַזֶּה

And he said to them,
"*Now* listen to this dream."

---

1. The ה ָ ending also appears with the Imperfect, Consecutive Imperfect, and Infinitive Construct.

Qal Imperative Paradigms: Weak Verbs

Most weak Imperative verbs are derived from the corresponding Imperfect forms, minus the Imperfect preformative. There are some weak forms that do not correspond exactly to their Imperfect counterparts.

	I-Guttural	II-Guttural	I-א (Type 1)	I-א (Type 2)
2ms	חֲזַק	בְּחַר	אֱמֹר	אֱסֹר
2fs	חִזְקִי	בַּחֲרִי	אִמְרִי	אִסְרִי
2mp	חִזְקוּ	בַּחֲרוּ	אִמְרוּ	אִסְרוּ
2fp	חֲזַ֫קְנָה	בְּחַ֫רְנָה	אֱמֹ֫רְנָה	אֱסֹ֫רְנָה

	III-א	III-ח/ע	III-ה	Geminate
2ms	מְצָא	שְׁלַח	בְּנֵה	סֹב
2fs	מִצְאִי	שִׁלְחִי	בְּנִי	סֹ֫בִּי
2mp	מִצְאוּ	שִׁלְחוּ	בְּנוּ	סֹ֫בּוּ
2fp	מְצֶ֫אנָה	שְׁלַ֫חְנָה	בְּנֶ֫ינָה	סֹ֫בְנָה

	I-נ (Type 2)	I-נ (Type 1)	I-י (Type 2)	I-י (Type 1)
2ms	סַע	נְפֹל	רַשׁ	שֵׁב
2fs	סְעִי	נִפְלִי	רְשִׁי	שְׁבִי
2mp	סְעוּ	נִפְלוּ	רְשׁוּ	שְׁבוּ
2fp	סַ֫עְנָה	נְפֹ֫לְנָה	רַ֫שְׁנָה	שֵׁ֫בְנָה

	Bicon	נָתַן	הָלַךְ	לָקַח
2ms	קוּם	תֵּן	לֵךְ	קַח
2fs	ק֫וּמִי	תְּנִי	לְכִי	קְחִי
2mp	ק֫וּמוּ	תְּנוּ	לְכוּ	קְחוּ
2fp	קֹ֫מְנָה	תֵּ֫נָּה	לֵ֫כְנָה	קַ֫חְנָה

Qal Imperative Paradigms: Weak Verb Notes

1. With III-ה Verbs, the 2ms form ends with Tsere He (בְּנֵה). The other three forms lack this final vowel letter (e.g., 2mp בְּנוּ).
2. With Geminate verbs, the 2fs and 2mp forms appear with Daghesh Forte in the remaining Geminate consonant (ס֫בִּי and ס֫בּוּ).
3. With I-נ (Type 2) and I-י verbs, the initial weak root letter does not appear in any of the Imperative forms (e.g., סַע and שֵׁב).
4. Biconsonatal verbs appear with their medial vowel letters (e.g., ק֫וּמוּ), except in the 2fp (קֹ֫מְנָה).
5. Remember that the verb הָלַךְ inflects like a I-י verb, and that the verb לָקַח inflects like a I-נ verb.

QAL INFINITIVE CONSTRUCT

Qal Infinitive Construct: Strong Verbs

The Infinitive Construct form is not inflected for person, gender, or number. There is, therefore, only one basic form:

קְטֹל

Notes: Strong Verbs

1. The Qal Infinitive Construct form is identical to the Qal Imperative 2ms (also קְטֹל). The Imperative is common in discourse (speech), frequently the first word in its clause. The Infinitive Construct can be distinguished by the regular appearance of a prepositional prefix (e.g., לִזְכֹּר).
2. The Infinitive Construct frequently appears with a pronominal suffix that can function as either the subject or object of the verbal idea. When appearing with a pronominal suffix, the spelling of the Qal Infinitive Construct is קָטְל (with Qamets Hatuf), as in קָטְלוֹ.
3. The negative particles לֹא and אַל are not used to negate the Infinitive Construct. Rather, the Hebrew Infinitive is negated with בִּלְתִּי (or לְבִלְתִּי) meaning "not" or "in order not."

לְבִלְתִּי אֱכֹל

(in order) not to eat

Qal Infinitive Construct: Weak Verbs

The vowel pattern for the Qal Infinitive Construct is consistent for all strong verbs and many weak verbs. Below, the Qal Infinitive Construct appears with the Qal Imperative for comparison. Note the consistent presence of the o-class stem vowel (Holem) throughout the forms of the Qal Infinitive Construct.

	Imperative 2ms	Infinitive Construct
Strong	שְׁמֹר	שְׁמֹר
Strong	זְכֹר	זְכֹר
Strong	שְׁפֹךְ	שְׁפֹךְ
I-Gutt	עֲזֹב	עֲזֹב
I-א	אֱמֹר	אֱמֹר
II-Gutt	בְּחַר	בְּחֹר
III-ח	שְׁלַח	שְׁלֹחַ
III-ע	שְׁמַע	שְׁמֹעַ
III-א	קְרָא	קְרֹא

Qal Infinitive Construct: III-ה Verbs

The Infinitive Construct form of III-ה verbs ends in וֹת. Vocal Shewa appears under the first root letter (or a Hateph vowel with gutturals). In the following chart, several III-ה verbs are listed in their Infinitive Construct form.

Lexical Form	Infinitive Construct	Lexical Form	Infinitive Construct
בָּנָה	בְּנוֹת	עָשָׂה	עֲשׂוֹת
בָּכָה	בְּכוֹת	הָיָה	הֱיוֹת
עָלָה	עֲלוֹת	רָאָה	רְאוֹת
עָנָה	עֲנוֹת	שָׁתָה	שְׁתוֹת

Qal Infinitive Construct: I-נ Verbs

Many I-נ verbs have Infinitive Construct forms that conform to the strong verb pattern, as in נְפֹל or נְסֹעַ. Some I-נ verbs, however, drop the initial נ and add ת to the end, as in סַ֫עַת (from נָסַע). This alternate form is rendered as a Segholate and, therefore, accented on the first syllable.

Lexical Form	Strong Pattern	Alternate Pattern
נָגַשׁ		גֶּ֫שֶׁת
נָסַע	נְסֹעַ	סַ֫עַת
נָגַע	נְגֹעַ	גַּ֫עַת
נָתַן	נְתֹן	תֵּת[1]
נָשָׂא	נְשֹׂא	שְׂאֵת[2]

---

1. This Infinitive Construct form has lost both its first and third root consonants through assimilation.
2. Variation in vowel pattern is occasioned by the quiescent א in the third root position.

Qal Infinitive Construct: I-י Verbs

A few I-י verbs preserve the strong vowel pattern as in יְשֹׁן from יָשֵׁן. However, most I-י verbs drop the initial י and add a final ת (just like I-נ verbs). This alternate form is also rendered as a Segholate and, therefore, accented on the first syllable.

Lexical Form	Infinitive Construct	Lexical Form	Infinitive Construct
יָשַׁב	שֶׁ֫בֶת	יָצָא	צֵאת[3]
יָרַשׁ	רֶ֫שֶׁת	הָלַךְ	לֶ֫כֶת[4]
יָלַד	לֶ֫דֶת	יָדַע	דַּ֫עַת[5]

Qal Infinitive Construct: Biconsonantal Verbs

Biconsonantal verbs are divided into three classes based on their medial vowel letter: קוּם with Shureq, בּוֹא with Holem Waw, and שִׂים with Hireq Yod. These lexical forms are, in fact, the Infinitive Construct forms (also identical to Imperative 2ms). Additional examples include: מוּת and שׁוּב and בּוֹשׁ and דִּין.

---

3. Variation in vowel pattern is occasioned by the quiescent א in third root position.
4. The verb הָלַךְ inflects like a I-י verb.
5. Variation in vowel pattern (Pathach instead of Seghol) is occasioned by the guttural consonant in the third root position.

Syntax of the Infinitive Construct

1. **Purpose, Intention, or Result**. When prefixed with the preposition לְ, the Infinitive Construct may denote purpose, intention, or result. The key words "to" or "in order to" may be used in translation.

   וַיֵּשְׁבוּ לֶאֱכָל־לֶחֶם

   And they sat down *(in order) to eat* bread.

   וְלֹא־נָתַן יְהוָה לָכֶם לֵב לָדַעַת
   וְעֵינַיִם לִרְאוֹת וְאָזְנַיִם לִשְׁמֹעַ

   But Yahweh has not given to you
   a heart *to know* or eyes *to see* or ears *to hear*.

2. **Inceptive**. When prefixed with the preposition לְ, the Infinitive Construct may denote an action about to take place. This construction frequently involves the use of הָיָה (to be). The key words "about to" may be used in your translation.

   וַיְהִי הַשֶּׁמֶשׁ לָבוֹא

   The sun was *about to set*.

   וַיְהִי הַשַּׁעַר לִסְגּוֹר

   The gate was *about to shut*.

3. **Verbal Noun**. The Infinitive Construct may function like a noun, often as the subject or object of the verbal idea. It may or may not be prefixed with the preposition לְ.

הִנֵּה שְׁמֹעַ מִזֶּבַח טוֹב

Behold, *to obey* is better than sacrifice.

טוֹב לְהֹדוֹת לַיהוָה

It is good *to praise* Yahweh.

4. **Complementary**. The Infinitive Construct may explain, clarify, or complement a preceding action or statement. It may or may not be prefixed with the preposition לְ. With this use, translate the Infinitive Construct with "by" plus the "-ing" form of the verb.

וְשָׁמְרוּ בְנֵי־יִשְׂרָאֵל אֶת־הַשַּׁבָּת לַעֲשׂוֹת
אֶת־הַשַּׁבָּת לְדֹרֹתָם בְּרִית עוֹלָם

The people of Israel shall observe the Sabbath *by doing* the Sabbath throughout their generations as an everlasting covenant.

וְלֹא־הָיִיתָ כְּעַבְדִּי דָוִד אֲשֶׁר שָׁמַר מִצְוֹתַי וַאֲשֶׁר־הָלַךְ
אַחֲרַי בְּכָל־לְבָבוֹ לַעֲשׂוֹת רַק הַיָּשָׁר בְּעֵינָי

You were not like my servant David who observed my commandments and who walked after me with all his heart *by doing* only what was right in my eyes.

5. **Temporal**. When prefixed with the prepositions בְּ or כְּ, the Infinitive Construct may be used in a temporal clause. When used in this way, the prepositions בְּ and כְּ are translated as either "when" or "while." Frequently, in this construction, the Infinitive Construct will also have a pronominal suffix.

וַיְהִי בִּשְׁכֹּן יִשְׂרָאֵל בָּאָרֶץ הַהִוא

And it was *when* Israel *dwelt* in that land . . .

וְהָיָה כְּצֵאת מֹשֶׁה אֶל־הָאֹהֶל יָקוּמוּ כָּל־הָעָם

And it would be *when* Moses *went out* to the tent, all the people would rise up.

Note that the temporal modifiers וַיְהִי and וְהָיָה provide the context for determining the temporal value of the Infinitive Construct. The temporal modifier וַיְהִי signals past tense narration and the temporal modifier וְהָיָה signals future tense narration. Of course, there are other contextual considerations that will help to determine the tense value.

QAL INFINITIVE ABSOLUTE

Qal Infinitive Absolute: Strong Verbs

The Infinitive Absolute form is not inflected for person, gender, or number. There is only one basic form:

קָטוֹל

Notes: Strong Verbs

1. The Holem Waw stem vowel may be written defectively as Holem (e.g., קָטֹל).
2. Do not confuse the alternate form of the Infinitive Absolute (קָטֹל) with the Imperative 2ms or Infinitive Construct verb forms (קְטֹל). The Qamets under the first root consonant will distinguish the Infinitive Absolute.
3. Unlike the Infinitive Construct, the Infinitive Absolute does not occur with prepositional prefixes or pronominal suffixes.

Qal Infinitive Absolute: Weak Verbs

The vowel pattern of the strong verb also occurs in most weak verb types.

	Perfect 3ms	Infinitive Absolute	Defective Spelling
I-Guttural	אָכַל	אָכוֹל	אָכֹל
II-Guttural	בָּחַר	בָּחוֹר	בָּחֹר

	Perfect 3ms	Infinitive Absolute	Defective Spelling
III-ח/ע	שָׁכַח	שָׁכוֹחַ	שָׁכֹחַ
III-א	יָצָא	יָצוֹא	יָצֹא
I-נ	נָתַן	נָתוֹן	נָתֹן
I-י	יָדַע	יָדוֹעַ	יָדֹעַ
Geminate	סָבַב	סָבוֹב	סָבֹב

Qal Infinitive Absolute: III-ה Verbs

With III-ה verbs, the Infinitive Absolute may appear in one of two forms.

Lexical Form	Option 1	Option 2
עָשָׂה	עָשֹׂה	עָשׂוֹ
שָׁתָה	שָׁתֹה	שָׁתוֹ
רָאָה	רָאֹה	רָאוֹ
חָיָה	חָיֹה	חָיוֹ

Qal Infinitive Absolute: Biconsonatal Verbs

With Biconsonantal verbs, the Infinitive Absolute appears with a Holem Waw (or Holem) stem vowel in every class.

Lexical Form	Infinitive Absolute	Lexical Form	Infinitive Absolute
בּוֹא	בּוֹא	קוּם	קוֹם
שִׂים	שׂוֹם	מוּת	מוֹת

Syntax of the Infinitive Absolute

Like the Infinitive Construct, the Infinitive Absolute is also a verbal noun. With regard to function, however, there is no precise English equivalent to the Hebrew Infinitive Absolute. Remember that the Infinitive Absolute does not occur with prepositional prefixes or pronominal suffixes.

1. **Emphatic**. The Infinitive Absolute may precede (or follow) a Perfect or Imperfect verbal form of the same root in order to highlight the certainty of the verbal action.

    שָׁמוֹעַ תִּשְׁמְעוּ
    You will *indeed* listen.

    מוֹת תָּמוּת
    You will *certainly* die.

2. **Imperatival**. The Infinitive Absolute can stand by itself and function as an Imperative.

    זָכוֹר אֶת־הַיּוֹם הַזֶּה
    Remember this day!

    שָׁמוֹר אֶת־יוֹם הַשַּׁבָּת
    Observe the sabbath day!

3. **Contemporaneous**. Two Infinitive Absolutes may be used together with a Perfect or Imperfect verb for the purpose of expressing two verbal actions occurring simultaneously.

וַיֵּלֶךְ הָלוֹךְ וְאָכֹל

And he walked, *eating as he went*.

וְעָלוּ עָלֹה וּבָכֹה

And they went up, *weeping as they went*.

4. **Complementary**. An Infinitive Absolute may complement the main verb of a sentence and carry the temporal value of that main verb. In this usage, the Infinitive Absolute will translate just like a Perfect or Imperfect even though it is not an inflected form.

מוֹת יוּמַת הָאִישׁ
רָגוֹם אֹתוֹ בָאֲבָנִים כָּל־הָעֵדָה

The man *shall* certainly *be put to death*;
all of the congregation *shall stone*
him with stones.

וַיַּרְכֵּב אֹתוֹ בְּמִרְכֶּבֶת הַמִּשְׁנֶה . . .
וְנָתוֹן אֹתוֹ עַל כָּל־אֶרֶץ מִצְרָיִם

And he made him ride in the second chariot . . .
and *he set him* over all the land of Egypt.

QAL ACTIVE PARTICIPLE

The Participle is a verbal adjective, and so it shares characteristics with both verbs and adjectives. As a verb, the Participle has stem (Qal) and voice (active or passive) and expresses some type of verbal action, such as "running" or "studying." As an adjective, the Participle has gender and number, and it is used much like an adjective: attributively, predicatively, and substantively.

Strong Verbs

The active Participle inflects like an adjective, with both gender and number. It is not inflected for person. Note that there are two feminine singular forms.

	Singular	Plural
Masculine	קֹטֵל	קֹטְלִים
Feminine	קֹטְלָה	קֹטְלוֹת
Feminine	קֹטֶ֫לֶת	

Notes:

1. The Holem vowel in the first syllable is diagnostic of the active Qal Participle. This vowel will not reduce and it appears in all strong and weak verb forms (except Biconsonantal). The Holem may also be written as Holem Waw (קוֹטֵל).
2. The feminine singular form קֹטֶ֫לֶת is more common than קֹטְלָה.

3. Because Participles behave like adjectives, they may take the definite article, prepositional prefixes, or pronominal suffixes. They may also appear in the construct state.

Weak Verbs

In the Qal stem, I-Guttural, I-נ, I-י, and Geminate verbs follow the strong verb pattern. Other weak verbal roots deviate slightly from this strong verb pattern. Note that in every weak verb class except one (Biconsonantal), the diagnostic Holem vowel and inflectional endings are unchanged.

1. **II-Guttural**. With a guttural in second root position, Vocal Shewa will appear as Hateph Pathach in the fs, mp, and fp forms.

	Singular	Plural
Masculine	בֹּחֵר	בֹּחֲרִים
Feminine	בֹּחֲרָה	בֹּחֲרוֹת
Feminine	בֹּחֶ֫רֶת	

2. **III-ח/ע**. In this weak verb class, only the feminine singular form (שֹׁמַ֫עַת) varies from the strong verb pattern (קֹטֶ֫לֶת). This change is due to the fact that gutturals prefer a-class vowels.

	Singular	Plural
Masculine	שֹׁמֵעַ	שֹׁמְעִים
Feminine	שֹׁמְעָה	שֹׁמְעוֹת
Feminine	שֹׁמַ֫עַת	

3. **III-א**. Only the feminine singular form מֹצֵאת varies from the strong verb pattern. In this form, the א is quiescent. The remaining III-א forms follow the strong verb pattern.

	Singular	Plural
Masculine	מֹצֵא	מֹצְאִים
Feminine	מֹצְאָה	מֹצְאוֹת
Feminine	מֹצֵאת	

4. **III-ה**. In this weak class, the final root consonant (ה) is lost in every form. Be careful to distinguish between the masculine singular בֹּנֶה and the feminine singular בֹּנָה. The Yod that appears in the feminine form בֹּנִיָּה reminds us that most III-ה verbs were originally III-י.

	Singular	Plural
Masculine	בֹּנֶה	בֹּנִים
Feminine	בֹּנָה	בֹּנוֹת
Feminine	בֹּנִיָּה	

5. **Biconsonantal**. Only this weak verb class appears without the diagnostic Holem vowel. Rather, the vowel in the first syllable will be Qamets. Note that the Qal Participle ms קָם (rising) is identical to the Qal Perfect 3ms form קָם (he rose). Likewise, the Qal Participle fs קָמָה (rising) is distinguished from the Qal Perfect 3fs form קָ֫מָה (she rose) only by the accent. Additionally, there is only one feminine singular form.

	Singular	Plural
Masculine	קָם	קָמִים
Feminine	קָמָה	קָמוֹת

Syntax of the Participle

In Hebrew, Participles function just like adjectives. As such, the three uses of the Participle are attributive, predicative, and substantive.

1. **Attributive**. When a Participle directly modifies a noun (e.g. "a *consuming* fire"), it is being used attributively. In Hebrew, this Participle will follow the noun that it modifies and agree in gender, number, and definiteness with that noun. The attributive Participle may also be translated with a relative clause (e.g., "a fire *that consumes*").

   הָעָם הַיֹּשֵׁב בָּאָרֶץ
   the people *who dwell* in the land

   יְהוָה אֱלֹהֶיךָ אֵשׁ אֹכְלָה
   Yahweh your God is a *consuming* fire.

2. **Predicative**. The predicative Participle asserts something about a noun, creating a predication (e.g. "the fire *is/was consuming*"). In English, a form of the verb "to be" is used to indicate the predicative relationship. In Hebrew, this participle will agree with the noun in gender and number, *but not in definiteness*. The predicative Participle never takes the definite article and usually follows the noun.

וְהָהָר בֹּעֵר בָּאֵשׁ

And the mountain *was burning* with fire.

וּשְׁמוּאֵל שֹׁכֵב בְּהֵיכַל

And Samuel *was lying down* in (the) temple.

3. **Substantive**. A Participle may be used independently as a noun, indicating the "one who" performs a certain action. In Hebrew, when a Participle is used substantively, it behaves just like a noun. As such, it may function as the subject or object of a verb, take a definite article, appear in a construct chain, or take pronominal suffixes and prepositional prefixes. In fact, several Hebrew Participles are used with such frequency as substantives that they are commonly listed as nouns. For example, the nouns **כֹּהֵן** (priest), **אֹיֵב** (enemy), and **שֹׁפֵט** (judge) are technically masculine singular Participles functioning substantively. A similar phenomenon occurs in English as well. For example, the "one who teaches" is called a "teacher" and the "one who studies" is called a "student."

הַיּוֹשֶׁבֶת בַּגַּנִּים

the one who dwells in the gardens

וְלֹא יִישָׁן שׁוֹמֵר יִשְׂרָאֵל

And *the one who keeps* Israel will not sleep.

QAL PASSIVE PARTICIPLE

In addition to the active Participle, the Qal stem also includes a passive Participle. The terms active and passive (voice) are used to describe the relationship between subject and verb. With verbs having an active voice, the subject of the verb performs the action of the verb (e.g., "David *killed* Goliath"). With verbs having a passive voice, the subject of the verb receives the verbal action (e.g., "Goliath *was killed* by David"). When translating a passive Participle, the "-ing" ending appears on the helping verb as in "*being* killed" or "*being* written." Additionally, an English form like "blessed" may be used, as in "*Blessed* is the person who studies Hebrew."

Strong Verbs

The passive Participle, like the active Participle, is inflected for gender and number. Unlike the active Participle, there is only one feminine singular form.

	Singular	Plural
Masculine	קָטוּל	קְטוּלִים
Feminine	קְטוּלָה	קְטוּלוֹת

Notes:

1. The Shureq stem vowel is diagnostic of the Qal passive Participle (קָטוּל). This vowel will not reduce and it appears in all strong and weak verb forms. The Shureq may also be written defectively as Qibbuts (קָטֻל).

2. In those forms with inflectional endings (fs, mp, fp), Vocal Shewa appears under the first root consonant, as in קְטוּלָה. The change from Qamets in the ms form (קָטוּל) to Vocal Shewa in the other forms is due to propretonic reduction, a common phenomenon in Hebrew morphology.

Weak Verbs

1. Many weak verbs maintain the strong verb diagnostics in the Qal passive Participle. Note the following examples:

Weak Class	Passive Participle	Weak Class	Passive Participle
I-Guttural	עָזוּב	I-י	יָדוּעַ
II-Guttural	שָׁאוּל	I-נ	נָטוּעַ
III-א	שָׂנוּא	Geminate	אָרוּר
III-ח/ע	פָּתוּחַ		

2. **I-Guttural**. With a guttural consonant in first root position, the Vocal Shewa in the inflected forms changes to Hateph Pathach. This occurs because gutturals cannot take Vocal Shewa, but take reduced vowels, usually Hateph Pathach.

	Singular	Plural
Masculine	עָזוּב	עֲזוּבִים
Feminine	עֲזוּבָה	עֲזוּבוֹת

3. **III-ה**. The forms of the Qal passive Participle for III-ה verbs require special attention. In every form, the *consonant* Yod stands in the place of the third root consonant, reminiscent of the fact that most III-ה verbs were originally III-י. Think of this Yod as diagnostic of the III-ה weak verb class. Knowing this will help to reconstruct the lexical form.

	Singular	Plural
Masculine	בָּנוּי	בְּנוּיִים
Feminine	בְּנוּיָה	בְּנוּיוֹת

Syntax of the Participle

The passive Qal Participle is used just like the active Qal Participle: attributively, predicatively, or substantively.

1. **Attributive**. The Participle follows the noun it modifies and agrees in gender, number, and definiteness.

הַבְּרִית הַכְּתוּבָה בְּסֵפֶר הַתּוֹרָה הַזֶּה
the covenant *written* in this book of the law

וַיִּבֶן אֶת־כָּל־הַחוֹמָה הַפְּרוּצָה
And he (re)built all of the *broken* wall.

2. **Predicative**. The Participle either precedes or follows the noun it modifies and agrees in gender and number, *but not definiteness*.

בָּרוּךְ יְהוָה לְעוֹלָם
Blessed is Yahweh forever.

אֲרוּרָה הָאֲדָמָה בַּעֲבוּרֶךָ

Cursed is the ground because of you.

3. **Substantive**. The Participle is used independently as a noun, indicating the "one who" performs a certain action. When a Participle is used substantively, it behaves just like a noun.

וְהֶחָלוּץ יַעֲבֹר לִפְנֵי אֲרוֹן יְהוָה

And *the one equipped* (for battle)
will pass before the ark of Yahweh.

וְתַחַת הֲרוּגִים יִפֹּלוּ

And they will fall among *the slain ones*.

NIPHAL STEM VERBS

Meaning of the Niphal Stem

In general, the Niphal (נִפְעַל) stem is used to express *simple action* with either a *passive* or *reflexive voice*. The Niphal stem may also express a *reciprocal* nuance. Additionally, some verbs that appear in the Niphal stem express the active voice of the Qal stem.

1. **Passive**. The Niphal stem may be used to express a simple action with a *passive voice*.

   Qal שָׁמַע he heard — Niphal נִשְׁמַע he *was* heard

2. **Reflexive**. The Niphal stem may be used to express a simple action with a *reflexive voice*.

   Qal שָׁמַע he heard — Niphal נִשְׁמַע he heard *himself*

3. **Reciprocal**. The Niphal stem may be used to express a simple action with a *reciprocal* nuance.

   Qal שָׁמְעוּ they heard — Niphal נִשְׁמְעוּ they heard *one another*

4. **Simple Active**. The Niphal stem may be used to express a simple action with an *active voice*, just like the Qal stem. Verbs of this type are commonly inflected in the Niphal stem and are rare or unattested in the Qal stem. Examples include: לָחַם (to fight), נָבָא (to prophecy), שָׁבַע (to swear), and שָׁאַר (to remain).

Niphal Stem Paradigms: Strong Verbs

Perfect	Imperfect	Imperative	Participle
נִקְטַל	יִקָּטֵל	הִקָּטֵל	נִקְטָל
נִקְטְלָה	תִּקָּטֵל	הִקָּטְלִי	נִקְטֶלֶת
נִקְטַלְתָּ	תִּקָּטֵל	הִקָּטְלוּ	נִקְטָלִים
נִקְטַלְתְּ	תִּקָּטְלִי	הִקָּטַלְנָה	נִקְטָלוֹת
נִקְטַלְתִּי	אֶקָּטֵל		
נִקְטְלוּ	יִקָּטְלוּ	**Inf Construct**	**Inf Absolute**
נִקְטַלְתֶּם	תִּקָּטַלְנָה	הִקָּטֵל	נִקְטוֹל
נִקְטַלְתֶּן	תִּקָּטְלוּ		הִקָּטוֹל
נִקְטַלְנוּ	תִּקָּטַלְנָה		
	נִקָּטֵל		

Notes: Niphal Stem with Strong Verbs

1. The primary diagnostic feature of the Niphal stem is the נִ prefix added to the verbal stem of every form. In the Perfect, Participle, and one form of the Infinitive Absolute, the נִ prefix is clearly present (e.g., נִקְטַל). In the Imperfect, Imperative, Infinitive Construct, and the other Infinitive Absolute form, the נ of Niphal stem prefix assimilates to the first consonant of the verbal root and remains as Daghesh Forte (e.g., יִקָּטֵל).

2. In the Imperfect conjugation, the נ of the Niphal stem assimilates to the first consonant of the verbal root. This assimilated נ is represented by Daghesh Forte in each form of the conjugation (e.g., יִקָּטֵל). The combination of the Hireq preformative vowel, the Qamets under the first root letter of every form, and the Daghesh Forte of the assimilated נ (e.g., יִקָּטֵל) clearly distinguishes the Niphal Imperfect from other Imperfect verbal forms.

3. In the Imperative, Infinite Construct, and one form of the Infinitive Absolute (הִקָּטוֹל), the נ of the Niphal stem has assimilated, and the consonant ה has been prefixed to the verbal root, preserving the Niphal stem diagnostics (e.g., הִקָּטֵל).

4. Carefully note the difference between the Niphal Perfect 3ms (נִקְטַל) and the Niphal Participle ms (נִקְטָל). The stem vowel for the Perfect is Pathach, but Qamets for the Participle.

5. The Imperative 2ms and the Infinitive Construct are identical in form. When encountering this form, context will help distinguish between the two possibilities. In general, Imperative verbs appear in discourse (speech), usually as the first word, and the Niphal Infinitive Construct is prefixed with an inseparable preposition over 75 percent of the time.

6. Both forms of the Niphal Infinitive Absolute are distinguished by the Holem Waw stem vowel: נִקְטוֹל and הִקָּטוֹל.

Niphal Stem Diagnostics: Strong and Weak Verbs

	Perfect	Imperfect	Imperative
Strong	נִקְטַל	יִקָּטֵל	הִקָּטֵל
III-א	נִמְצָא	יִמָּצֵא	הִמָּצֵא
III-ה	נִבְנָה	יִבָּנֶה	הִבָּנֵה
I-Guttural	נֶעֱזַב	יֵעָזֵב	הֵעָזֵב
I-נ	נִצַּל	יִנָּצֵל	הִנָּצֵל
I-י	נוֹשַׁב	יִוָּשֵׁב	הִוָּשֵׁב

	Infinitive Construct	Infinitive Absolute	Participle
Strong	הִקָּטֵל	נִקְטוֹל הִקָּטוֹל	נִקְטָל
III-א	הִמָּצֵא	נִמְצוֹא	נִמְצָא
III-ה	הִבָּנוֹת	נִבְנֹה הִבָּנֵה	נִבְנֶה
I-Guttural	הֵעָזֵב	נַעֲזוֹב הֵעָזוֹב	נֶעֱזָב
I-נ	הִנָּצֵל	הִנָּצֵל נִצּוֹל	נִצָּל
I-י	הִוָּשֵׁב		נוֹשָׁב

Notes: Niphal Stem Diagnostics

1. With III-ה verbs, most of the strong verb diagnostics remain. Simply note that the distinctive endings of III-ה verbs appearing with Qal stem verbs also appear with the Niphal and every other derived stem.

Diagnostic Endings for III-ה Verbs in All Stems

Perfect	ָה
Imperfect	ֶה
Imperative	ֵה
Infinitive Construct	וֹת
Participle	ֶה

2. With I-Guttural verbs, the prefix vowel in the Perfect, Participle, and one form of the Infinitive Absolute is variable between Seghol and Pathach: נֶעֱזָב, נֶעֱזַב, and נַעֲזוֹב. With the Imperfect, Imperative, Infinitive Construct, and the other form of the Infinitive Absolute, the Guttural in first root position rejects the Daghesh Forte of the assimilating נ and the Hireq prefix or preformative vowel lengthens to Tsere according to the rules for compensatory lengthening: יֵעָזֵב , הֵעָזֵב, and הֵעָזוֹב.

3. With I-נ verbs, the נ of the *verbal root* assimilates to the second consonant of the verbal root as Daghesh Forte in the Perfect, Participle, and one

form of the Infinitive Absolute: נִצַּל, נִצָּל, and נִצּוֹל. In spite of this weakness in the verbal root, the Niphal stem strong verb diagnostics are preserved. In the remaining I-נ conjugations, the נ of the verbal root does *not* assimilate and so these verbal forms exhibit the strong verb pattern.

4. I-י verbs were originally I-ו. In the Niphal stem, the original ו reappears in every form. In the Perfect and Participle, the original ו reappears as Holem Waw: נוֹשַׁב and נוֹשָׁב. With the Imperfect, Imperative, and Infinitive Construct, the original ו reappears as a consonant: יִוָּשֵׁב and הִוָּשֵׁב. Note that the נ of the Niphal stem appears as Daghesh Forte with the consonant ו. In these forms, all strong verb diagnostics are preserved. Recognition of the ו as diagnostic of the I-י weak verb class is essential for identification of the verbal root.

HIPHIL STEM VERBS

Meaning of the Hiphil Stem

In general, the Hiphil (הִפְעִיל) stem is used to express *causative types action* with an *active voice*.

1. **Causative**. The Hiphil stem is used to express *causative* action with an *active* voice.

   Qal מָלַךְ he reigned — Hiphil הִמְלִיךְ he made (someone) king

2. **Declarative**. Hiphil verbs sometimes carry a declarative nuance, meaning that the subject of the verb declares someone (or something) to be in a certain condition or state of being.

   Qal רָשַׁע he is guilty — Hiphil הִרְשִׁיעַ he declared (pronounced) guilty

3. **Factitive**. Like the Piel stem, the Hiphil stem may be used to make an intransitive verb (does not take a direct object) into a transitive verb (can take a direct object).

   Qal גָּדַל he is great — Hiphil הִגְדִּיל he made (someone) great

4. **Simple Action**. Some verbs in the Hiphil stem can express the simple action of the Qal stem. In this case, the Hiphil verb would be translated like a Qal verb. This is frequently the case with verbal roots that are common in the Hiphil stem but are not attested (or rarely attested) in the Qal stem.

Qal	שָׁכַם	Hiphil	הִשְׁכִּים
	**not attested*		he arose early

Hiphil Stem: Strong Verbs

Perfect	Imperfect	Imperative	Participle
הִקְטִיל	יַקְטִיל	הַקְטֵל	מַקְטִיל
הִקְטִ֫ילָה	תַּקְטִיל	הַקְטִ֫ילִי	מַקְטֶ֫לֶת
הִקְטַ֫לְתָּ	תַּקְטִיל	הַקְטִ֫ילוּ	מַקְטִילִים
הִקְטַלְתְּ	תַּקְטִ֫ילִי	הַקְטֵ֫לְנָה	מַקְטִילוֹת
הִקְטַ֫לְתִּי	אַקְטִיל		
הִקְטִ֫ילוּ	יַקְטִ֫ילוּ	**Inf Construct**	**Inf Absolute**
הִקְטַלְתֶּם	תַּקְטֵ֫לְנָה	הַקְטִיל	הַקְטֵל
הִקְטַלְתֶּן	תַּקְטִ֫ילוּ		
הִקְטַ֫לְנוּ	תַּקְטֵ֫לְנָה		
	נַקְטִיל		

Notes: Hiphil Stem with Strong Verbs

1. The most important diagnostic features of the Hiphil stem include: (1) ה prefix in all conjugations, except the Imperfect and Participle; (2) Pathach under all preformatives and prefixes, except in the Perfect; (3) Hireq Yod or Tsere stem vowel in all forms, except the second and first person forms of the Perfect.

2. The Perfect conjugation of the Hiphil stem is distinguished by the הִ prefix on every form (e.g., הִקְטִיל). In all third person forms, the stem vowel is Hireq Yod (e.g., הִקְטִיל). In all second and first person forms, the stem vowel is Pathach (e.g., הִקְטַ֫לְתָּ).

3. The Imperfect conjugation of the Hiphil stem is distinguished by a Pathach preformative vowel in every form (e.g., יַקְטִיל). The stem vowel is Hireq Yod throughout, except for the 3fp/2fp form (תַּקְטֵ֫לְנָה). When prefixed with Waw Consecutive, the stem vowel is usually Tsere and not Hireq Yod. Thus, יַקְטִיל becomes וַיַּקְטֵל.

4. The Imperative, Infinitive Construct, and Infinitive Absolute forms are distinguished by the הַ prefix on every form (e.g., הַקְטֵל). The stem vowels are variable between Hireq Yod and Tsere.

5. The Hiphil Participle appears with the מַ prefix in every form (e.g., מַקְטִיל). There are two feminine singular forms, מַקְטֶ֫לֶת and מַקְטִילָה. This same prefix also occurs with the Participles in all of the derived stems, except for the Niphal.

Hiphil Stem Diagnostics: Strong and Weak Verbs

	Perfect	Imperfect	Imperative
Strong	הִקְטִיל	יַקְטִיל	הַקְטֵל
I-Guttural	הֶעֱמִיד	יַעֲמִיד	הַעֲמֵד
III-ה	הִגְלָה	יַגְלֶה	הַגְלֵה
I-נ	הִצִּיל	יַצִּיל	הַצֵּל
I-י	הוֹשִׁיב	יוֹשִׁיב	הוֹשֵׁב
Bicon	הֵקִים	יָקִים	הָקֵם

	Infinitive Construct	Infinitive Absolute	Participle
Strong	הַקְטִיל	הַקְטֵל	מַקְטִיל
I-Guttural	הַעֲמִיד	הַעֲמֵד	מַעֲמִיד
III-ה	הַגְלוֹת	הַגְלֵה	מַגְלֶה
I-נ	הַצִּיל	הַצֵּל	מַצִּיל
I-י	הוֹשִׁיב	הוֹשֵׁב	מוֹשִׁיב
Bicon	הָקִים	הָקֵם	מֵקִים

Notes: Hiphil Stem Diagnostics for Weak Verbs

1. While not represented in the summary chart above, note that the stem vowel in the Perfect is variable between Hireq Yod and Pathach. In all other conjugations, the stem vowel varies between Hireq Yod and Tsere.
2. In the I-Guttural weak verb class, all of the strong verb diagnostics are present, except in the Perfect, where the prefix vowel is Seghol (הֶעֱמִיד).
3. In III-ה verbs, all prefix and preformative consonants and vowels retain the Hiphil strong verb diagnostics. Variation from the strong verb diagnostics occurs mainly in the stem vowels of the various conjugations, given the distinctive endings of III-ה verbs.

Diagnostic Endings for III-ה Verbs in All Stems

Perfect	ָה
Imperfect	ֶה
Imperative	ֵה
Infinitive Construct	וֹת
Participle	ֶה

4. With I-נ verbs, all strong verb diagnostics are present (e.g., הִצִּיל). The Daghesh Forte in the second root consonant (e.g., הִצִּיל) of every form represents the assimilated נ of the verbal root. Proper identification of the Daghesh Forte is necessary in order to reconstruct the verbal root.

5. With I-י verbs, the Yod in first root position has been replaced with Holem Waw (e.g., הוֹשִׁיב). In every conjugation, this Holem Waw follows the prefix or preformative consonant. As in the Niphal Perfect and Participle, the Holem Waw represents the reappearance of the Waw that was originally in first root position. Knowing that this Holem Waw is diagnostic of the I-י verb class will enable you to reconstruct the verbal root.

6. There are three Biconsonantal verb classes, each distinguished by their medial vowel letter: קוּם (with Shureq), שִׂים (with Hireq Yod), and בּוֹא (with Holem Waw). In the Hiphil stem, all Biconsonantal verbs exhibit the diagnostic Hireq Yod or Tsere stem vowel, regardless of the original Biconsonantal verb class. In the Perfect and Participle, the prefix vowel is Tsere (e.g., הֵקִים and מֵקִים) instead of Hireq (e.g., הִקְטִיל) or Pathach (e.g., מַקְטִיל). In the remaining Biconsonantal conjugations, the prefix vowel is Qamets (e.g., יָקִים) instead of Pathach (e.g., יַקְטִיל). Finally, note that all prefix and preformative vowels may reduce to Vocal Shewa or Hateph Pathach according to the rules of propretonic reduction, as in הֲקִימֹותִי (Hiphil Perfect 3ms), תְּקִימֶינָה (Hiphil Imperfect 2fp/3fp), or מְקִימִים (Qal Participle mp).

HOPHAL STEM VERBS

Meaning of the Hophal Stem

The Hophal (הָפְעַל) stem is the passive counterpart of the Hiphil stem. The Hophal stem is used, therefore, to express *causative types of action* with a *passive voice*. For example, the Hiphil Perfect verb הֵמִית means "he put to death." The Hophal form, however, would be הוּמָת, and it would be translated "he *was* put to death." A form of the English verb "to be" (was) is used to make the translation passive.

Hophal Stem: Strong Verbs

Perfect (U)	Perfect (O)	Imperfect (U)	Imperfect (O)
הֻקְטַל	הָקְטַל	יֻקְטַל	יָקְטַל
הֻקְטְלָה	הָקְטְלָה	תֻּקְטַל	תָּקְטַל
הֻקְטַלְתָּ	הָקְטַלְתָּ	תֻּקְטַל	תָּקְטַל
הֻקְטַלְתְּ	הָקְטַלְתְּ	תֻּקְטְלִי	תָּקְטְלִי
הֻקְטַלְתִּי	הָקְטַלְתִּי	אֻקְטַל	אָקְטַל
הֻקְטְלוּ	הָקְטְלוּ	יֻקְטְלוּ	יָקְטְלוּ
הֻקְטַלְתֶּם	הָקְטַלְתֶּם	תֻּקְטַלְנָה	תָּקְטַלְנָה
הֻקְטַלְתֶּן	הָקְטַלְתֶּן	תֻּקְטְלוּ	תָּקְטְלוּ
הֻקְטַלְנוּ	הָקְטַלְנוּ	תֻּקְטַלְנָה	תָּקְטַלְנָה
		נֻקְטַל	נָקְטַל

Participle (U)	Participle (O)
מֻקְטָל	מָקְטָל
מֻקְטֶלֶת	מָקְטֶלֶת
מֻקְטָלִים	מָקְטָלִים
מֻקְטָלוֹת	מָקְטָלוֹת

Notes: Hophal Stem with Strong Verbs

1. Because of their infrequency in the Hebrew Bible, the Hophal Imperative, Infinitive Construct, and Infinitive Absolute forms do not appear in the paradigms listed above.

2. The Hophal paradigms presented above appear in sets of two, with each set distinguished by the prefix vowel. The Hophal prefix vowel is variable between u-class and o-class vowels. With u-class vowels, Qibbuts appears most frequently (e.g., הֻקְטַל), but Shureq also occurs in many weak verbs. With o-class vowels, Qamets Hatuf occurs most frequently (e.g., הָקְטַל), but Holem and Holem Waw also appear. Thinking of the Hophal prefix vowel in terms of vowel classes (u-class *or* o-class) will prevent confusion when you encounter variation, especially with weak verbs.

3. In the Perfect and Imperfect conjugations, the stem vowel is Pathach (e.g., הָקְטַל), except in those forms with sufformatives that begin with or consist of a vowel (e.g., הָקְטְלָה). In the Participle, the stem vowel is Qamets (e.g.,מָקְטָל), except in the feminine singular.

4. The Hophal Participle also exhibits the מ prefix (מָקְטָל) associated with most of the derived stems.

Hophal Stem Diagnostics: Strong and Weak Verbs

	Perfect	Imperfect	Participle
Strong (U)	הֻקְטַל	יֻקְטַל	מֻקְטָל
Strong (O)	הָקְטַל	יָקְטַל	מָקְטָל
I-Guttural	הָעֳמַד	יָעֳמַד	מָעֳמָד
I-נ	הֻצַּל	יֻצַּל	מֻצָּל
III-ה	הָגְלָה	יָגְלֶה	מָגְלֶה
I-י	הוּשַׁב	יוּשַׁב	מוּשָׁב
Bicon	הוּקַם	יוּקַם	מוּקָם
Geminate	הוּסַב	יוּסַב	מוּסָב

Notes: Hophal Stem Diagnostics for Weak Verbs

1. In the I-Guttural and I-נ categories, all of the strong verb diagnostics of the Hophal stem are preserved. With I-נ verbs, the Daghesh Forte in the second root consonant (e.g., הֻצַּל) represents the assimilated נ of the verbal root (as in Hiphil).

2. With III-ה verbs, the prefix and preformative consonants and vowels exhibit the strong verb pattern. However, these verbs employ the

distinctive endings of III-ה verbs in each conjugation. In other words, verbs in this category are identified as Hophal by how they begin, and as III-ה by how they end.

Diagnostic Endings for III-ה Verbs in the Hophal Stem

Perfect	ָה
Imperfect	ֶה
Participle	ֶה

3. Weak verb diagnostics for I-י, Biconsonantal, and Geminate verbs in the Hophal stem are identical. In each case, the prefix or preformative vowel is Shureq (e.g., הוּשַׁב, but also spelled הֻשַּׁב). The stem vowels maintain the strong verb pattern: Pathach in the Perfect and Imperfect (e.g. הוּקַם) and Qamets in the Participle (e.g. מוּקָם). With these three weak verb classes in the Hophal stem, proper identification of the verbal root is achieved by a process of elimination. For example, in Gen 42:28 the silver of Joseph's brothers is described as הוּשַׁב. This inflected form is properly identified as Hophal Perfect 3ms, but from what verbal root: יָשַׁב (to sit), שׁוּב (to return), שָׁבַב (to cut down)? Was the silver "cut down" or "inhabited" (יָשַׁב in the Hophal stem)? Probably not. The best answer in this context is שׁוּב, the silver was "returned" or "given back." Remember, context is king!

PIEL STEM VERBS

Meaning of the Piel Stem

In general, the Piel (פִּעֵל) stem is used to express *intensive types of action* with an *active voice*.

1. **Intensive**. The Piel stem may be used to express *intensive* action with an *active* voice.

Qal	שָׁבַר he broke	Piel	שִׁבֵּר he smashed
	שָׁלַח he sent		שִׁלַּח he expelled

2. **Factitive**. The factitive use of the Piel makes an intransitive (does not take a direct object) Qal verb into *transitive* (can take a direct object) verb.

Qal	קָדַשׁ he was holy	Piel	קִדַּשׁ he sanctified
	אָבַד he perished		אִבַּד he destroyed

3. **Denominative**. Verbs that are *derived from a noun* or adjective are often inflected in the Piel stem, not the Qal. When this occurs, the type of verbal action is simple and not intensive.

Noun	דָּבָר word	Piel	דִּבֶּר he spoke
	עָפָר dust		עִפַּר he threw dirt

4. **Iterative**. The iterative action of the Piel expresses the nuance of *repeated action*. This use occurs primarily with verbs that express physical movement, effort, or voice projection.

Qal	הָלַךְ he walked	Piel	הִלֵּךְ he paced back and forth
	צָעַק he cried		צִעֵק he wept over and over, kept crying

5. **Simple Action**. Some verbs in the Piel stem are translated just like verbs in the Qal. This is frequently the case with verbal roots that are common in the Piel stem but are not attested (or rarely attested) in the Qal.

Qal	צָוָה *not attested*	Piel	צִוָּה he commanded
	בָּרַךְ he blessed		בֵּרֵךְ he blessed

Piel Stem: Strong Verbs

Perfect	Imperfect	Imperative	Participle
קִטֵּל	יְקַטֵּל	קַטֵּל	מְקַטֵּל
קִטְּלָה	תְּקַטֵּל	קַטְּלִי	מְקַטֶּלֶת
קִטַּלְתָּ	תְּקַטֵּל	קַטְּלוּ	מְקַטְּלִים
קִטַּלְתְּ	תְּקַטְּלִי	קַטֵּלְנָה	מְקַטְּלוֹת
קִטַּלְתִּי	אֲקַטֵּל		
קִטְּלוּ	יְקַטְּלוּ	**Inf Construct**	**Inf Absolute**
קִטַּלְתֶּם	תְּקַטֵּלְנָה	קַטֵּל	קַטֵּל
קִטַּלְתֶּן	תְּקַטְּלוּ		
קִטַּלְנוּ	תְּקַטֵּלְנָה		
	נְקַטֵּל		

Notes: Piel Stem with Strong Verbs

1. The most important diagnostic features for the strong verb of the Piel stem include: (1) Daghesh Forte in the second root consonant of every form; (2) Pathach under the first root consonant of every conjugation, except the Perfect; and (3) Vocal Shewa under all Imperfect and Participle preformatives and prefixes. Though not considered to be diagnostic, it is helpful to note the Tsere stem vowel throughout the conjugations.

2. The Perfect conjugation of the Piel stem is distinguished by Hireq under the first root letter and Daghesh Forte in the second root letter (e.g., קִטֵּל).

3. In every conjugation of the Piel stem, except the Perfect, the vowel under the first root letter is Pathach (e.g., יְקַטֵּל and מְקַטֵּל).

4. The preformative vowel in the Imperfect (יְקַטֵּל) and the prefix vowel in the Participle (מְקַטֵּל) is always Vocal Shewa (except in the Imperfect 1cs, אֲקַטֵּל).

5. The Imperative 2ms, Infinitive Construct, and Infinitive Absolute are identical in form (קַטֵּל). In context, these forms are easily distinguished from each other.

6. Note the distinctive מ prefix in the forms of the Piel Participle (e.g., מְקַטֵּל). This same prefix also occurs with the Participles in all of the derived stems, except for the Niphal.

Piel Stem Diagnostics: Strong and Weak Verbs

	Perfect	Imperfect	Imperative
Strong	קִטֵּל	יְקַטֵּל	קַטֵּל
III-ח/ע	שִׁלַּח	יְשַׁלַּח	שַׁלַּח
III-א	מִצֵּא	יְמַצֵּא	מַצֵּא
III-ה	גִּלָּה	יְגַלֶּה	גַּלֵּה
Geminate	הִלֵּל	יְהַלֵּל	הַלֵּל
II-Guttural	נִחַם	יְנַחֵם	נַחֵם
II-Guttural	בֵּרֵךְ	יְבָרֵךְ	בָּרֵךְ

	Infinitive Construct	Infinitive Absolute	Participle
Strong	קַטֵּל	קַטֵּל	מְקַטֵּל
III-ח/ע	שַׁלַּח	שַׁלֵּחַ	מְשַׁלֵּחַ
III-א	מַצֵּא	מַצֹּא	מְמַצֵּא
III-ה	גַּלּוֹת	גַּלֵּה	מְגַלֶּה
Geminate	הַלֵּל	הַלֵּל	מְהַלֵּל
II-Guttural	נַחֵם	נַחֵם	מְנַחֵם
II-Guttural	בָּרֵךְ	בָּרֵךְ	מְבָרֵךְ

Notes: Piel Stem Diagnostics for Weak Verbs

1. With Piel stem verbs, the strong verb diagnostics are preserved in each of the weak verb classes presented above, except for the II-Guttural weak verb class.

2. With II-Guttural verbs, the Daghesh Forte of the Piel stem is rejected by the guttural consonant in the second root position. The rejection of this Daghesh Forte results in either virtual doubling (e.g., יְנַחֵם) or compensatory lengthening (e.g., יְבָרֵךְ). With *virtual doubling*, the Daghesh Forte is rejected, but Pathach (short *a*) does *not* lengthen to Qamets (long *a*). With *compensatory lengthening*, Pathach lengthens to Qamets in each form.

3. With III-ה verbs, all of the strong verb diagnostics remain. Simply note that the distinctive endings of III-ה continue to appear with Piel stem verbs.

Diagnostic Endings for III-ה Verbs in All Stems

Perfect	ָה
Imperfect	ֶה
Imperative	ֵה
Infinitive Construct	וֹת
Participle	ֶה

Loss of Daghesh Forte

Sqnmlwy. This acronym identifies all "s" type consonants in Hebrew (ס ,צ ,שׂ, and שׁ), plus the letters q (ק), n (נ), m (מ), l (ל), w (ו), and y (י). When one of these letters appears with a Daghesh Forte *and* a Vocal Shewa, the Daghesh Forte will frequently drop out (e.g., הַמְּרַגְּלִים becomes הַמְרַגְּלִים or וַיְּהִי becomes וַיְהִי). This is the *sqnmlwy* phenomenon and it is especially common with the Piel stem, as the following examples illustrate.

1. הַמְדַבֵּר – Piel Participle ms with the definite article. The expected Daghesh Forte of the definite article is lost because the syllable begins with מְ.
2. וַיְדַבֵּר — Piel Imperfect 3ms with Waw Consecutive. The expected Daghesh Forte of the Waw Consecutive is lost because the syllable begins with יְ.
3. וַיְקַנְאוּ – Piel Imperfect 3mp with Waw Consecutive. The expected Daghesh Forte of the Waw Consecutive is lost because the syllable begins with יְ. Additionally, the expected Daghesh Forte in the second root consonant of the Piel stem is absent because נ is one of the consonants that may give up a Daghesh Forte when occurring with Vocal Shewa (נְ).
4. מִלְאוּ – Piel Perfect 3cp. The expected Daghesh Forte in the second root consonant of the Piel stem is lost because the ל occurs with Vocal Shewa (לְ).

PUAL STEM VERBS

Meaning of the Pual Stem

The Pual (פֻּעַל) stem is the passive counterpart of the Piel stem. The Pual stem is used, therefore, to express *intensive types of action* with a *passive voice*. For example, the Piel Perfect verb שִׁבֵּר means "he smashed." The Pual form, however, would be שֻׁבַּר, and it would be translated "he (it) *was* smashed." A form of the English verb "to be" (was) is used to make the translation passive.

Pual Stem: Strong Verbs

Perfect	Imperfect	Participle
קֻטַּל	יְקֻטַּל	מְקֻטָּל
קֻטְּלָה	תְּקֻטַּל	מְקֻטֶּלֶת
קֻטַּלְתָּ	תְּקֻטַּל	מְקֻטָּלִים
קֻטַּלְתְּ	תְּקֻטְּלִי	מְקֻטָּלוֹת
קֻטַּלְתִּי	אֲקֻטַּל	
קֻטְּלוּ	יְקֻטְּלוּ	
קֻטַּלְתֶּם	תְּקֻטַּלְנָה	
קֻטַּלְתֶּן	תְּקֻטְּלוּ	
קֻטַּלְנוּ	תְּקֻטַּלְנָה	
	נְקֻטַּל	

Notes: Pual Stem with Strong Verbs

1. Because of their infrequency in the Hebrew Bible, the Pual Imperative, Infinitive Construct, and Infinitive Absolute forms do not appear in the paradigms listed above.

2. The diagnostic features for the strong verb of the Pual stem include: (1) Daghesh Forte in the second root consonant of *every* form; (2) Qibbuts under the first root consonant of *every* conjugation; and (3) Vocal Shewa under *all* Imperfect and Participle preformatives and prefixes.

3. The Qibbuts vowel under the first root letter of each form in every conjugation distinguishes the Pual stem (e.g., יְקֻטַּל) from the Piel stem (יְקַטֵּל).

4. The preformative vowel in the Imperfect (יְקֻטַּל) and the prefix vowel in the Participle (מְקֻטָּל) is always Vocal Shewa (except in the Imperfect 1cs, אֲקֻטַּל).

5. The Daghesh Forte appearing in the second root letter of every form in the Pual stem is also diagnostic of the Piel and Hithpael stems.

6. Note the distinctive מ prefix in the forms of the Pual Participle (e.g., מְקֻטָּל). This same prefix also occurs with the Participles in all of the derived stems, except for the Niphal.

Pual Stem Diagnostics: Strong and Weak Verbs

	Perfect	Imperfect	Participle
Strong	קֻטַּל	יְקֻטַּל	מְקֻטָּל
III-א	מֻצָּא	יְמֻצָּא	מְמֻצָּא
III-ה	גֻּלָּה	יְגֻלֶּה	מְגֻלֶּה
II-Guttural	נֻחַם	יְנֻחַם	מְנֻחָם
II-Guttural	בֹּרַךְ	יְבֹרַךְ	מְבֹרָךְ

Notes: Pual Stem Diagnostics for Weak Verbs

1. With Pual stem verbs, the strong verb diagnostics are preserved in each of the weak verb classes, except for the II-Guttural weak verb class.

2. With II-Guttural verbs, the Daghesh Forte of the Pual stem is rejected by the guttural consonant in second root position. The rejection of this Daghesh Forte results in either virtual doubling (e.g., יְנֻחַם) or compensatory lengthening (e.g., יְבֹרַךְ). With *virtual doubling*, the Daghesh Forte is rejected, but Qibbuts (short *u*) does *not* lengthen to Holem (long *o*). With *compensatory lengthening*, Qibbuts lengthens to Holem in each form.

3. With III-ה verbs, all of the strong verb diagnostics remain. Simply note that the distinctive endings of III-ה continue to appear with Pual stem verbs.

HITHPAEL STEM VERBS

Meaning of the Hithpael Stem

In general, the Hithpael (הִתְפַּעֵל) stem is used to express *intensive types of action* with a *reflexive voice.*

1. **Reflexive**. The Hithpael stem may be used to express an *intensive* type of action with a *reflexive* voice.

Qal	קָדַשׁ he was holy	Hithpael	הִתְקַדֵּשׁ he sanctified *himself*

2. **Reciprocal**. This type of action expresses the nuance of reciprocity, or mutual action.

Qal	רָאָה he saw	Hithpael	הִתְרָאוּ they looked *at each other*

3. **Iterative**. The iterative expresses the notion of repeated action.

Noun	הָלַךְ he walked	Hithpael	הִתְהַלֵּךְ he paced *back and forth*

4. **Simple Action**. With some verbs, the Hithpael stem is best translated just like the Qal: simple action with an active voice.

Qal	פָּלַל **not attested*	Hithpael	הִתְפַּלֵּל he prayed

Hithpael Stem: Strong Verbs

Perfect	Imperfect	Imperative	Participle
הִתְקַטֵּל	יִתְקַטֵּל	הִתְקַטֵּל	מִתְקַטֵּל
הִתְקַטְּלָה	תִּתְקַטֵּל	הִתְקַטְּלִי	מִתְקַטֶּלֶת
הִתְקַטַּלְתָּ	תִּתְקַטֵּל	הִתְקַטְּלוּ	מִתְקַטְּלִים
הִתְקַטַּלְתְּ	תִּתְקַטְּלִי	הִתְקַטֵּלְנָה	מִתְקַטְּלוֹת
הִתְקַטַּלְתִּי	אֶתְקַטֵּל		
הִתְקַטְּלוּ	יִתְקַטְּלוּ		
הִתְקַטַּלְתֶּם	תִּתְקַטֵּלְנָה		
הִתְקַטַּלְתֶּן	תִּתְקַטְּלוּ		
הִתְקַטַּלְנוּ	תִּתְקַטֵּלְנָה		
	נִתְקַטֵּל		

Inf Construct	Inf Absolute
הִתְקַטֵּל	הִתְקַטֵּל

Notes: Hithpael Stem with Strong Verbs

1. The diagnostic features of the Hithpael stem include: (1) הִתְ prefix; (2) Pathach under the first consonant of the verbal root; and (3) Daghesh Forte in the second consonant of the verbal root. With expected variations, these diagnostic features appear in every conjugation of the Hithpael strong verb.

2. In the Imperfect, the ה of the Hithpael prefix has dropped out and the Imperfect preformative appears in its place. So, for example, יְהִתְ has become יִתְ (or תִּתְ or אֶתְ or נִתְ).

3. In the Participle, the ה of the Hithpael prefix has dropped out and the Participle prefix (מ) appears in its place. In other words, מְהִתְ has become מִתְ.

4. The Perfect 3ms, Imperative 2ms, Infinitive Construct, and Infinitive Absolute are identical in form and diagnostics (הִתְקַטֵּל). In most contexts, these forms are readily distinguished.

Hithpael Stem Diagnostics: Strong and Weak Verbs

	Perfect	Imperfect	Imperative
Strong	הִתְקַטֵּל	יִתְקַטֵּל	הִתְקַטֵּל
III-ה	הִתְגַּלָּה	יִתְגַּלֶּה	הִתְגַּלֵּה
II-Guttural	הִתְנַחֵם	יִתְנַחֵם	הִתְנַחֵם
II-Guttural	הִתְבָּרֵךְ	יִתְבָּרֵךְ	הִתְבָּרֵךְ

	Infinitive Construct	Infinitive Absolute	Participle
Strong	הִתְקַטֵּל	הִתְקַטֵּל	מִתְקַטֵּל
III-ה	הִתְגַּלּוֹת		מִתְגַּלֶּה
II-Guttural	הִתְנַחֵם	הִתְנַחֵם	מִתְנַחֵם
II-Guttural	הִתְבָּרֵךְ	הִתְבָּרֵךְ	מִתְבָּרֵךְ

Notes: Hithpael Stem Diagnostics for Weak Verbs

1. With Hithpael stem verbs, the strong verb diagnostics are preserved in many of the weak verb classes. The II-Guttural weak verb class, however, requires special attention.

2. With II-Guttural verbs, the Daghesh Forte of the Hithpael stem is rejected by the guttural consonant in second root position. The rejection of this Daghesh Forte results in either virtual doubling (e.g., הִתְנַחֵם) or compensatory lengthening (e.g., הִתְבָּרֵךְ). With *virtual doubling*, the Daghesh Forte is rejected, but Pathach (short *a*) does *not* lengthen to Qamets (long *a*). With *compensatory lengthening*, Pathach lengthens to Qamets in each form.

3. With III-ה verbs, all of the strong verb diagnostics remain. Simply note that the distinctive endings of III-ה continue to appear with Hithpael stem verbs.

Diagnostic Endings for III-ה Verbs in All Stems

Perfect	◌ָה
Imperfect	◌ֶה
Imperative	◌ֵה
Infinitive Construct	וֹת
Participle	◌ֶה

Metathesis in the Hithpael Stem

Metathesis describes the transposition of two contiguous (side-by-side) consonants in order to smooth out a word's pronunciation. In Hebrew, whenever the ת of the Hithpael prefix precedes verbal roots beginning with ס, צ, שׁ, or שׂ (sibilant or "s" sound consonants), the two consonants will switch places.

סָתַר	he hid	הִסְתַּתֵּר	he hid himself
שָׁמַר	he kept	הִשְׁתַּמֵּר	he kept himself
צָדֵק	he is just	הִצְטַדֵּק[1]	he justified himself

Assimilation of ת in the Hithpael Stem

When the first consonant of a verbal root is ד, ז, ט, or ת, the ת of the Hithpael prefix will assimilate into the first consonant of the verbal root and appear as Daghesh Forte.

דָּבַר	he spoke	הִדַּבֵּר	he spoke with
טָמֵא	he is unclean	הִטַּמֵּא	he became unclean

1. When the first consonant of the verbal root is צ, the ת of the Hithpael prefix will switch places with the first consonant of the verbal root. Additionally, the ת of the Hithpael prefix changes to ט: הִתְצַדֵּק becomes הִצְטַדֵּק.

OTHER DERIVED STEMS

In addition to the seven "major" stems of the Hebrew verbal system (Qal and the six derived stems), there are a number of additional stems that are considered "minor" because of their relative infrequency. Four of these minor stems are described below (Polel, Polal, Hithpolel, and Hishtaphel).

Polel Stem

Perfect	Imperfect	Imperative	Participle
רוֹמֵם	יְרוֹמֵם	רוֹמֵם	מְרוֹמֵם
רוֹמְמָה	תְּרוֹמֵם	רוֹמְמִי	מְרוֹמֶ֫מֶת
רוֹמַ֫מְתָּ	תְּרוֹמֵם	רוֹמְמוּ	מְרוֹמְמִים
רוֹמַמְתְּ	תְּרוֹמְמִי	רוֹמֵ֫מְנָה	מְרוֹמְמוֹת
רוֹמַ֫מְתִּי	אֲרוֹמֵם		
רוֹמְמוּ	יְרוֹמְמוּ	**Inf Construct**	
רוֹמַמְתֶּם	תְּרוֹמֵ֫מְנָה	רוֹמֵם	
רוֹמַמְתֶּן	תְּרוֹמְמוּ		
רוֹמַ֫מְנוּ	תְּרוֹמֵ֫מְנָה		
	נְרוֹמֵם		

Notes: Polel Stem

1. Biconsonantal verbs (e.g., רוּם) occur infrequently in the Piel stem. Instead, they occur in the Polel stem. Geminate roots may also appear in this stem. In general, the meaning of the Piel corresponds to the meaning of the Polel.

2. Biconsonantal verbs in the Polel stem are distinguished by Holem Waw after the first root consonant (e.g., רוֹמֵם) and duplication of the second root consonant (e.g., רוֹמֵם). The preformative and the prefix vowel is Vocal Shewa (e.g., יְרוֹמֵם).

Polal Stem

Perfect	Imperfect	Participle
רוֹמַם	יְרוֹמַם	מְרוֹמָם
רוֹמְמָה	תְּרוֹמַם	מְרוֹמֶ֫מֶת
רוֹמַ֫מְתָּ	תְּרוֹמַם	מְרוֹמָמִים
רוֹמַמְתְּ	תְּרוֹמְמִי	מְרוֹמָמוֹת
רוֹמַ֫מְתִּי	אֲרוֹמַם	
רוֹמְמוּ	יְרוֹמְמוּ	
רוֹמַמְתֶּם	תְּרוֹמַ֫מְנָה	
רוֹמַמְתֶּן	תְּרוֹמְמוּ	
רוֹמַ֫מְנוּ	תְּרוֹמַ֫מְנָה	
	נְרוֹמַם	

Notes: Polal Stem

1. The Polal stem is the passive counterpart of the Polel. It is the equivalent of the Pual stem for certain Biconsonantal (and Geminate) verbal roots.

2. The diagnostic features of the Polal stem are identical to the Polel stem: (1) Holem Waw after the first root consonant; (2) duplication of the second root consonant; and (3) Vocal Shewa preformative and prefix vowel. The Polal (רוֹמַם) is distinguished from the Polel (רוֹמֵם) by its stem vowel.

Hithpolel Stem

Perfect	Imperfect	Imperative	Participle
הִתְרוֹמֵם	יִתְרוֹמֵם	הִתְרוֹמֵם	מִתְרוֹמֵם
הִתְרוֹמְמָה	תִּתְרוֹמֵם	הִתְרוֹמְמִי	מִתְרוֹמֶ֫מֶת
הִתְרוֹמַ֫מְתָּ	תִּתְרוֹמֵם	הִתְרוֹמְמוּ	מִתְרוֹמְמִים
הִתְרוֹמַמְתְּ	תִּתְרוֹמְמִי	הִתְרוֹמֵ֫מְנָה	מִתְרוֹמְמוֹת
הִתְרוֹמַ֫מְתִּי	אֶתְרוֹמֵם		
הִתְרוֹמְמוּ	יִתְרוֹמְמוּ	**Inf Construct**	
הִתְרוֹמַמְתֶּם	תִּתְרוֹמֵ֫מְנָה	הִתְרוֹמֵם	
הִתְרוֹמַמְתֶּן	תִּתְרוֹמְמוּ		
הִתְרוֹמַ֫מְנוּ	תִּתְרוֹמֵ֫מְנָה		
	נִתְרוֹמֵם		

Notes: Hithpolel Stem

1. The Hithpolel stem is the reflexive counterpart of the Polel stem. It is the equivalent of the Hithpael stem for certain Biconsonantal (and Geminate) verbal roots.

2. The diagnostic features of the Hithpolel stem include: (1) הִתְ prefix; (2) Holem Waw after the first root consonant; (3) duplication of the second root consonant; and (4) Vocal Shewa preformative and prefix vowel.

3. In the Imperfect, the ה of the Hithpolel prefix has dropped out and the Imperfect preformative appears in its place. So, for example, יְהִתְ has become יִתְ (or תִּתְ or אֶתְ or נִתְ).

4. In the Participle, the ה of the Hithpolel prefix has dropped out and the Participle prefix (מ) appears in its place. In other words, מְהִתְ has become מִתְ.

Hishtaphel Stem

Perfect

הִשְׁתַּחֲוָה	3ms	he worshiped
הִשְׁתַּחֲווּ	3cp	they worshiped
הִשְׁתַּחֲוִיתֶם	2mp	you worshiped

Imperfect

יִשְׁתַּחֲוֶה	3ms	he will worship
וַיִּשְׁתַּחוּ	3ms	he worshiped (Waw Consecutive)
תִּשְׁתַּחֲוֶה	2ms	you will worship
אֶשְׁתַּחֲוֶה	1cs	I will worship
יִשְׁתַּחֲווּ	3mp	they will worship

Imperative

הִשְׁתַּחֲווּ	2mp	worship!

Infinitive Construct

הִשְׁתַּחֲוֹת		to worship

Participle

מִשְׁתַּחֲוֶה	ms	worshiping
מִשְׁתַּחֲוִים	mp	worshiping

Notes: Hishtaphel Stem

1. The verb חָוָה (to bow down, worship) appears 173 times in the Hebrew Bible. This verb occurs only in the Hishtaphel stem, and the Hishtaphel stem occurs only with this verb.

2. The diagnostic feature of the Hishtaphel is the stem prefix הִשְׁתַּ. This distinctive stem prefix appears with every form.

3. In the Imperfect, the ה of the Hishtaphel prefix has dropped out and the Imperfect preformative appears in its place. So, for example, יְהִשְׁתַּ has become יִשְׁתַּ (or תִּשְׁתַּ or אֶשְׁתַּ).

4. In the Participle, the ה of the Hishtaphel prefix has dropped out and the Participle prefix (מ) appears in its place. In other words, מְהִשְׁתַּ has become מִשְׁתַּ.

5. חָוָה is a III-ה verb and will exhibit the distinctive endings of this weak verb class.

Diagnostic Endings for III-ה Verbs in All Stems

Perfect	ָה
Imperfect	ֶה
Imperative	ֵה
Infinitive Construct	וֹת
Participle	ֶה

VERB PARADIGMS AND CHARTS

Qal Perfect: Strong and Stative Verbs

	Pathach	Tsere	Holem	Strong
3ms	גָּדַל	כָּבֵד	קָטֹן	קָטַל
3fs	גָּֽדְלָה	כָּֽבְדָה	קָֽטְנָה	קָֽטְלָה
2ms	גָּדַלְתָּ	כָּבַדְתָּ	קָטֹנְתָּ	קָטַלְתָּ
2fs	גָּדַלְתְּ	כָּבַדְתְּ	קָטֹנְתְּ	קָטַלְתְּ
1cs	גָּדַלְתִּי	כָּבַדְתִּי	קָטֹנְתִּי	קָטַלְתִּי
3cp	גָּֽדְלוּ	כָּֽבְדוּ	קָֽטְנוּ	קָֽטְלוּ
2mp	גְּדַלְתֶּם	כְּבַדְתֶּם	קְטָנְתֶּם	קְטַלְתֶּם
2fp	גְּדַלְתֶּן	כְּבַדְתֶּן	קְטָנְתֶּן	קְטַלְתֶּן
1cp	גָּדַלְנוּ	כָּבַדְנוּ	קָטֹנּוּ	קָטַלְנוּ

Qal Perfect: Weak Verbs 1

	I-Guttural	II-Guttural	III-ח/ע	III-א
3ms	עָמַד	בָּחַר	שָׁמַע	מָצָא
3fs	עָֽמְדָה	בָּֽחֲרָה	שָֽׁמְעָה	מָֽצְאָה
2ms	עָמַדְתָּ	בָּחַרְתָּ	שָׁמַעְתָּ	מָצָאתָ
2fs	עָמַדְתְּ	בָּחַרְתְּ	שָׁמַעַתְּ	מָצָאת
1cs	עָמַדְתִּי	בָּחַרְתִּי	שָׁמַעְתִּי	מָצָאתִי
3cp	עָֽמְדוּ	בָּֽחֲרוּ	שָֽׁמְעוּ	מָֽצְאוּ
2mp	עֲמַדְתֶּם	בְּחַרְתֶּם	שְׁמַעְתֶּם	מְצָאתֶם
2fp	עֲמַדְתֶּן	בְּחַרְתֶּן	שְׁמַעְתֶּן	מְצָאתֶן
1cp	עָמַדְנוּ	בָּחַרְנוּ	שָׁמַעְנוּ	מָצָאנוּ

Qal Perfect: Weak Verbs 2

	III-ה	Biconsonantal	Geminate	I-Gutt/III-ה
3ms	בָּנָה	קָם	סָבַב	עָלָה
3fs	בָּֽנְתָה	קָ֫מָה	סָֽבְבָה	עָֽלְתָה
2ms	בָּנִ֫יתָ	קַ֫מְתָּ	סַבּ֫וֹתָ	עָלִ֫יתָ
2fs	בָּנִית	קַמְתְּ	סַבּוֹת	עָלִית
1cs	בָּנִ֫יתִי	קַ֫מְתִּי	סַבּ֫וֹתִי	עָלִ֫יתִי
3cp	בָּנוּ	קָ֫מוּ	סָֽבְבוּ	עָלוּ
2mp	בְּנִיתֶם	קַמְתֶּם	סַבּוֹתֶם	עֲלִיתֶם
2fp	בְּנִיתֶן	קַמְתֶּן	סַבּוֹתֶן	עֲלִיתֶן
1cp	בָּנִ֫ינוּ	קַ֫מְנוּ	סַבּ֫וֹנוּ	עָלִ֫ינוּ

Qal Imperfect: Strong and Stative Verbs

	Pathach	Tsere	Holem	Strong
3ms	יִגְדַּל	יִכְבַּד	יִקְטַן	יִקְטֹל
3fs	תִּגְדַּל	תִּכְבַּד	תִּקְטַן	תִּקְטֹל
2ms	תִּגְדַּל	תִּכְבַּד	תִּקְטַן	תִּקְטֹל
2fs	תִּגְדְּלִי	תִּכְבְּדִי	תִּקְטְנִי	תִּקְטְלִי
1cs	אֶגְדַּל	אֶכְבַּד	אֶקְטַן	אֶקְטֹל
3mp	יִגְדְּלוּ	יִכְבְּדוּ	יִקְטְנוּ	יִקְטְלוּ
3fp	תִּגְדַּ֫לְנָה	תִּכְבַּ֫דְנָה	תִּקְטַ֫נָּה	תִּקְטֹ֫לְנָה
2mp	תִּגְדְּלוּ	תִּכְבְּדוּ	תִּקְטְנוּ	תִּקְטְלוּ
2fp	תִּגְדַּ֫לְנָה	תִּכְבַּ֫דְנָה	תִּקְטַ֫נָּה	תִּקְטֹ֫לְנָה
1cp	נִגְדַּל	נִכְבַּד	נִקְטַן	נִקְטֹל

Qal Imperfect: Weak Verbs 1

	II-Guttural	III-ח/ע	III-א
3ms	יִבְחַר	יִשְׁלַח	יִמְצָא
3fs	תִּבְחַר	תִּשְׁלַח	תִּמְצָא
2ms	תִּבְחַר	תִּשְׁלַח	תִּמְצָא
2fs	תִּבְחֲרִי	תִּשְׁלְחִי	תִּמְצְאִי
1cs	אֶבְחַר	אֶשְׁלַח	אֶמְצָא
3mp	יִבְחֲרוּ	יִשְׁלְחוּ	יִמְצְאוּ
3fp	תִּבְחַ֫רְנָה	תִּשְׁלַ֫חְנָה	תִּמְצֶ֫אנָה
2mp	תִּבְחֲרוּ	תִּשְׁלְחוּ	תִּמְצְאוּ
2fp	תִּבְחַ֫רְנָה	תִּשְׁלַ֫חְנָה	תִּמְצֶ֫אנָה
1cp	נִבְחַר	נִשְׁלַח	נִמְצָא

Qal Imperfect: Weak Verbs 2

	I-Guttural (T1)	I-Guttural (T2)	I-א
3ms	יֶחֱזַק	יַעֲמֹד	יֹאמַר
3fs	תֶּחֱזַק	תַּעֲמֹד	תֹּאמַר
2ms	תֶּחֱזַק	תַּעֲמֹד	תֹּאמַר
2fs	תֶּחֶזְקִי	תַּעַמְדִי	תֹּאמְרִי
1cs	אֶחֱזַק	אֶעֱמֹד	אֹמַר
3mp	יֶחֶזְקוּ	יַעַמְדוּ	יֹאמְרוּ
3fp	תֶּחֱזַ֫קְנָה	תַּעֲמֹ֫דְנָה	תֹּאמַ֫רְנָה
2mp	תֶּחֶזְקוּ	תַּעַמְדוּ	תֹּאמְרוּ
2fp	תֶּחֱזַ֫קְנָה	תַּעֲמֹ֫דְנָה	תֹּאמַ֫רְנָה
1cp	נֶחֱזַק	נַעֲמֹד	נֹאמַר

Qal Imperfect: Weak Verbs 3 (Biconsonantal)

	קוּם	שִׂים	בּוֹא
3ms	יָקוּם	יָשִׂים	יָבוֹא
3fs	תָּקוּם	תָּשִׂים	תָּבוֹא
2ms	תָּקוּם	תָּשִׂים	תָּבוֹא
2fs	תָּקוּמִי	תָּשִׂימִי	תָּבוֹאִי
1cs	אָקוּם	אָשִׂים	אָבוֹא
3mp	יָקוּמוּ	יָשִׂימוּ	יָבוֹאוּ
3fp	תְּקוּמֶינָה	תְּשִׂימֶינָה	תָּבוֹאנָה
2mp	תָּקוּמוּ	תָּשִׂימוּ	תָּבוֹאוּ
2fp	תְּקוּמֶינָה	תְּשִׂימֶינָה	תָּבוֹאנָה
1cp	נָקוּם	נָשִׂים	נָבוֹא

Qal Imperfect: Weak Verbs 4

	III-ה	I-י	I-נ	Geminate
3ms	יִבְנֶה	יֵשֵׁב	יִפֹּל	יָסֹב
3fs	תִּבְנֶה	תֵּשֵׁב	תִּפֹּל	תָּסֹב
2ms	תִּבְנֶה	תֵּשֵׁב	תִּפֹּל	תָּסֹב
2fs	תִּבְנִי	תֵּשְׁבִי	תִּפְּלִי	תָּסֹבִּי
1cs	אֶבְנֶה	אֵשֵׁב	אֶפֹּל	אָסֹב
3mp	יִבְנוּ	יֵשְׁבוּ	יִפְּלוּ	יָסֹבּוּ
3fp	תִּבְנֶינָה	תֵּשַׁבְנָה	תִּפֹּלְנָה	תְּסֻבֶּינָה
2mp	תִּבְנוּ	תֵּשְׁבוּ	תִּפְּלוּ	תָּסֹבּוּ
2fp	תִּבְנֶינָה	תֵּשַׁבְנָה	תִּפֹּלְנָה	תְּסֻבֶּינָה
1cp	נִבְנֶה	נֵשֵׁב	נִפֹּל	נָסֹב

Qal Imperative: Weak Verbs

	I-Guttural	II-Guttural	I-א (T1)	I-א (T2)
2ms	חֲזַק	בְּחַר	אֱמֹר	אֱסֹר
2fs	חִזְקִי	בַּחֲרִי	אִמְרִי	אִסְרִי
2mp	חִזְקוּ	בַּחֲרוּ	אִמְרוּ	אִסְרוּ
2fp	חֲזַ֫קְנָה	בְּחַ֫רְנָה	אֱמֹ֫רְנָה	אֱסֹ֫רְנָה

	III-א	III-ח/ע	III-ה	Geminate
2ms	מְצָא	שְׁלַח	בְּנֵה	סֹב
2fs	מִצְאִי	שִׁלְחִי	בְּנִי	סֹ֫בִּי
2mp	מִצְאוּ	שִׁלְחוּ	בְּנוּ	סֹ֫בּוּ
2fp	מְצֶ֫אנָה	שְׁלַ֫חְנָה	בְּנֶ֫ינָה	סֹ֫בְנָה

	I-נ (T2)	I-נ (T1)	I-י (T2)	I-י (T1)
2ms	סַע	נְפֹל	רַשׁ	שֵׁב
2fs	סְעִי	נִפְלִי	רְשִׁי	שְׁבִי
2mp	סְעוּ	נִפְלוּ	רְשׁוּ	שְׁבוּ
2fp	סַ֫עְנָה	נְפֹ֫לְנָה	רַ֫שְׁנָה	שֵׁ֫בְנָה

	Bicon	נָתַן	הָלַךְ	לָקַח
2ms	קוּם	תֵּן	לֵךְ	קַח
2fs	ק֫וּמִי	תְּנִי	לְכִי	קְחִי
2mp	ק֫וּמוּ	תְּנוּ	לְכוּ	קְחוּ
2fp	קֹ֫מְנָה	תֵּ֫נָּה	לֵ֫כְנָה	קַ֫חְנָה

Qal Active Participle: Strong and Weak Verbs

	Strong	II-Guttural	III-ח/ע
ms	קֹטֵל	בֹּחֵר	שֹׁמֵעַ
mp	קֹטְלִים	בֹּחֲרִים	שֹׁמְעִים
fs	קֹטְלָה	בֹּחֲרָה	שֹׁמְעָה
fs	קֹטֶ֫לֶת	בֹּחֶ֫רֶת	שֹׁמַ֫עַת
fp	קֹטְלוֹת	בֹּחֲרוֹת	שֹׁמְעוֹת

	III-א	III-ה	Bicon
ms	מֹצֵא	בֹּנֶה	קָם
mp	מֹצְאִים	בֹּנִים	קָמִים
fs	מֹצְאָה	בֹּנָה	קָמָה
fs	מֹצֵאת	בֹּנִיָּה	
fp	מֹצְאוֹת	בֹּנוֹת	קָמוֹת

Qal Passive Participle: Strong and Weak Verbs

	Strong	I-Guttural	III-ה
ms	קָטוּל	עָזוּב	בָּנוּי
mp	קְטוּלִים	עֲזוּבִים	בְּנוּיִים
fs	קְטוּלָה	עֲזוּבָה	בְּנוּיָה
fp	קְטוּלוֹת	עֲזוּבוֹת	בְּנוּיוֹת

Niphal Stem: Strong Verbs

Perfect	Imperfect	Imperative	Participle
נִקְטַל	יִקָּטֵל	הִקָּטֵל	נִקְטָל
נִקְטְלָה	תִּקָּטֵל	הִקָּטְלִי	נִקְטֶלֶת
נִקְטַלְתָּ	תִּקָּטֵל	הִקָּטְלוּ	נִקְטָלִים
נִקְטַלְתְּ	תִּקָּטְלִי	הִקָּטַלְנָה	נִקְטָלוֹת
נִקְטַלְתִּי	אֶקָּטֵל		
נִקְטְלוּ	יִקָּטְלוּ	**Inf Construct**	**Inf Absolute**
נִקְטַלְתֶּם	תִּקָּטַלְנָה	הִקָּטֵל	נִקְטוֹל
נִקְטַלְתֶּן	תִּקָּטְלוּ		הִקָּטוֹל
נִקְטַלְנוּ	תִּקָּטַלְנָה		
	נִקָּטֵל		

Hiphil Stem: Strong Verbs

Perfect	Imperfect	Imperative	Participle
הִקְטִיל	יַקְטִיל	הַקְטֵל	מַקְטִיל
הִקְטִילָה	תַּקְטִיל	הַקְטִילִי	מַקְטֶלֶת
הִקְטַלְתָּ	תַּקְטִיל	הַקְטִילוּ	מַקְטִילִים
הִקְטַלְתְּ	תַּקְטִילִי	הַקְטֵלְנָה	מַקְטִילוֹת
הִקְטַלְתִּי	אַקְטִיל		
הִקְטִילוּ	יַקְטִילוּ	**Inf Construct**	**Inf Absolute**
הִקְטַלְתֶּם	תַּקְטֵלְנָה	הַקְטִיל	הַקְטֵל
הִקְטַלְתֶּן	תַּקְטִילוּ		
הִקְטַלְנוּ	תַּקְטֵלְנָה		
	נַקְטִיל		

Hophal Stem: Strong Verbs (u-class)

Perfect	Imperfect	Participle
הֻקְטַל	יֻקְטַל	מֻקְטָל
הֻקְטְלָה	תֻּקְטַל	מֻקְטֶ֫לֶת
הֻקְטַ֫לְתָּ	תֻּקְטַל	מֻקְטָלִים
הֻקְטַלְתְּ	תֻּקְטְלִי	מֻקְטָלוֹת
הֻקְטַ֫לְתִּי	אֻקְטַל	
הֻקְטְלוּ	יֻקְטְלוּ	
הֻקְטַלְתֶּם	תֻּקְטַ֫לְנָה	
הֻקְטַלְתֶּן	תֻּקְטְלוּ	
הֻקְטַ֫לְנוּ	תֻּקְטַ֫לְנָה	
	נֻקְטַל	

Hophal Stem: Strong Verbs (o-class)

Perfect	Imperfect	Participle
הָקְטַל	יָקְטַל	מָקְטָל
הָקְטְלָה	תָּקְטַל	מָקְטֶ֫לֶת
הָקְטַ֫לְתָּ	תָּקְטַל	מָקְטָלִים
הָקְטַלְתְּ	תָּקְטְלִי	מָקְטָלוֹת
הָקְטַ֫לְתִּי	אָקְטַל	
הָקְטְלוּ	יָקְטְלוּ	
הָקְטַלְתֶּם	תָּקְטַ֫לְנָה	
הָקְטַלְתֶּן	תָּקְטְלוּ	
הָקְטַ֫לְנוּ	תָּקְטַ֫לְנָה	
	נָקְטַל	

Piel Stem: Strong Verbs

Perfect	Imperfect	Imperative	Participle
קִטֵּל	יְקַטֵּל	קַטֵּל	מְקַטֵּל
קִטְּלָה	תְּקַטֵּל	קַטְּלִי	מְקַטֶּלֶת
קִטַּלְתָּ	תְּקַטֵּל	קַטְּלוּ	מְקַטְּלִים
קִטַּלְתְּ	תְּקַטְּלִי	קַטֵּלְנָה	מְקַטְּלוֹת
קִטַּלְתִּי	אֲקַטֵּל		
קִטְּלוּ	יְקַטְּלוּ	**Inf Construct**	**Inf Absolute**
קִטַּלְתֶּם	תְּקַטֵּלְנָה	קַטֵּל	קַטֵּל
קִטַּלְתֶּן	תְּקַטְּלוּ		
קִטַּלְנוּ	תְּקַטֵּלְנָה		
	נְקַטֵּל		

Pual Stem: Strong Verbs

Perfect	Imperfect	Participle
קֻטַּל	יְקֻטַּל	מְקֻטָּל
קֻטְּלָה	תְּקֻטַּל	מְקֻטֶּלֶת
קֻטַּלְתָּ	תְּקֻטַּל	מְקֻטָּלִים
קֻטַּלְתְּ	תְּקֻטְּלִי	מְקֻטָּלוֹת
קֻטַּלְתִּי	אֲקֻטַּל	
קֻטְּלוּ	יְקֻטְּלוּ	
קֻטַּלְתֶּם	תְּקֻטַּלְנָה	
קֻטַּלְתֶּן	תְּקֻטְּלוּ	
קֻטַּלְנוּ	תְּקֻטַּלְנָה	
	נְקֻטַּל	

Hithpael Stem: Strong Verbs

Perfect	Imperfect	Imperative	Participle
הִתְקַטֵּל	יִתְקַטֵּל	הִתְקַטֵּל	מִתְקַטֵּל
הִתְקַטְּלָה	תִּתְקַטֵּל	הִתְקַטְּלִי	מִתְקַטֶּ֫לֶת
הִתְקַטַּ֫לְתָּ	תִּתְקַטֵּל	הִתְקַטְּלוּ	מִתְקַטְּלִים
הִתְקַטַּלְתְּ	תִּתְקַטְּלִי	הִתְקַטֵּ֫לְנָה	מִתְקַטְּלוֹת
הִתְקַטַּ֫לְתִּי	אֶתְקַטֵּל		
הִתְקַטְּלוּ	יִתְקַטְּלוּ		
הִתְקַטַּלְתֶּם	תִּתְקַטֵּ֫לְנָה		
הִתְקַטַּלְתֶּן	תִּתְקַטְּלוּ		
הִתְקַטַּ֫לְנוּ	תִּתְקַטֵּ֫לְנָה		
	נִתְקַטֵּל		

Inf Construct	Inf Absolute
הִתְקַטֵּל	הִתְקַטֵּל

Niphal Stem Diagnostics: Strong and Weak Verbs

	Perfect	Imperfect	Imperative
Strong	נִקְטַל	יִקָּטֵל	הִקָּטֵל
III-א	נִמְצָא	יִמָּצֵא	הִמָּצֵא
III-ה	נִבְנָה	יִבָּנֶה	הִבָּנֵה
I-Guttural	נֶעֱזַב	יֵעָזֵב	הֵעָזֵב
I-נ	נִצַּל	יִנָּצֵל	הִנָּצֵל
I-י	נוֹשַׁב	יִוָּשֵׁב	הִוָּשֵׁב

	Infinitive Construct	Infinitive Absolute	Participle
Strong	הִקָּטֵל	נִקְטוֹל הִקָּטוֹל	נִקְטָל
III-א	הִמָּצֵא	נִמְצוֹא	נִמְצָא
III-ה	הִבָּנוֹת	נִבְנֹה הִבָּנֵה	נִבְנֶה
I-Guttural	הֵעָזֵב	נַעֲזוֹב הֵעָזוֹב	נֶעֱזָב
I-נ	הִנָּצֵל	הִנָּצֵל נִצּוֹל	נִצָּל
I-י	הִוָּשֵׁב		נוֹשָׁב

Hiphil Stem Diagnostics: Strong and Weak Verbs

	Perfect	Imperfect	Imperative
Strong	הִקְטִיל	יַקְטִיל	הַקְטֵל
I-Guttural	הֶעֱמִיד	יַעֲמִיד	הַעֲמֵד
III-ה	הִגְלָה	יַגְלֶה	הַגְלֵה
I-נ	הִצִּיל	יַצִּיל	הַצֵּל
I-י	הוֹשִׁיב	יוֹשִׁיב	הוֹשֵׁב
Bicon	הֵקִים	יָקִים	הָקֵם

	Infinitive Construct	Infinitive Absolute	Participle
Strong	הַקְטִיל	הַקְטֵל	מַקְטִיל
I-Guttural	הַעֲמִיד	הַעֲמֵד	מַעֲמִיד
III-ה	הַגְלוֹת	הַגְלֵה	מַגְלֶה
I-נ	הַצִּיל	הַצֵּל	מַצִּיל
I-י	הוֹשִׁיב	הוֹשֵׁב	מוֹשִׁיב
Bicon	הָקִים	הָקֵם	מֵקִים

Hophal Stem Diagnostics: Strong and Weak Verbs

	Perfect	Imperfect	Participle
Strong (U)	הֻקְטַל	יֻקְטַל	מֻקְטָל
Strong (O)	הָקְטַל	יָקְטַל	מָקְטָל
I-Guttural	הָעֳמַד	יָעֳמַד	מָעֳמָד
I-נ	הֻצַּל	יֻצַּל	מֻצָּל
III-ה	הָגְלָה	יָגְלֶה	מָגְלֶה
I-י	הוּשַׁב	יוּשַׁב	מוּשָׁב
Bicon	הוּקַם	יוּקַם	מוּקָם
Geminate	הוּסַב	יוּסַב	מוּסָב

Piel Stem Diagnostics: Strong and Weak Verbs

	Perfect	Imperfect	Imperative
Strong	קִטֵּל	יְקַטֵּל	קַטֵּל
III-ח/ע	שִׁלַּח	יְשַׁלַּח	שַׁלַּח
III-א	מִצֵּא	יְמַצֵּא	מַצֵּא
III-ה	גִּלָּה	יְגַלֶּה	גַּלֵּה
Geminate	הִלֵּל	יְהַלֵּל	הַלֵּל
II-Guttural	נִחַם	יְנַחֵם	נַחֵם
II-Guttural	בֵּרַךְ	יְבָרֵךְ	בָּרֵךְ

	Infinitive Construct	Infinitive Absolute	Participle
Strong	קַטֵּל	קַטֵּל	מְקַטֵּל
III-ח/ע	שַׁלַּח	שַׁלֵּחַ	מְשַׁלֵּחַ
III-א	מַצֵּא	מַצֹּא	מְמַצֵּא
III-ה	גַּלּוֹת	גַּלֵּה	מְגַלֶּה
Geminate	הַלֵּל	הַלֵּל	מְהַלֵּל
II-Guttural	נַחֵם	נַחֵם	מְנַחֵם
II-Guttural	בָּרֵךְ	בָּרֵךְ	מְבָרֵךְ

Pual Stem Diagnostics: Strong and Weak Verbs

	Perfect	Imperfect	Participle
Strong	קֻטַּל	יְקֻטַּל	מְקֻטָּל
III-א	מֻצָּא	יְמֻצָּא	מְמֻצָּא
III-ה	גֻּלָּה	יְגֻלֶּה	מְגֻלֶּה
II-Guttural	נֻחַם	יְנֻחַם	מְנֻחָם
II-Guttural	בֹּרַךְ	יְבֹרַךְ	מְבֹרָךְ

Hithpael Stem Diagnostics: Strong and Weak Verbs

	Perfect	Imperfect	Imperative
Strong	הִתְקַטֵּל	יִתְקַטֵּל	הִתְקַטֵּל
III-ה	הִתְגַּלָּה	יִתְגַּלֶּה	הִתְגַּלֵּה
II-Guttural	הִתְנַחֵם	יִתְנַחֵם	הִתְנַחֵם
II-Guttural	הִתְבָּרֵךְ	יִתְבָּרֵךְ	הִתְבָּרֵךְ

	Infinitive Construct	Infinitive Absolute	Participle
Strong	הִתְקַטֵּל	הִתְקַטֵּל	מִתְקַטֵּל
III-ה	הִתְגַּלּוֹת		מִתְגַּלֶּה
II-Guttural	הִתְנַחֵם	הִתְנַחֵם	מִתְנַחֵם
II-Guttural	הִתְבָּרֵךְ	הִתְבָּרֵךְ	מִתְבָּרֵךְ

HEBREW-ENGLISH LEXICON

א

אָב father, ancestor; (ms cstr) אֲבִי; (mp) אָבוֹת (1,210)

אָבַד (Q) to perish, vanish, be(come) lost, go astray; (Pi) cause to perish, destroy; (Hi) exterminate (185)

אָבָה (Q) to be willing, consent, yield to, want something (54)

אֶבְיוֹן (adj) poor, needy (61)

אַבִּיר (adj) mighty, strong, powerful (17)

אֵ֫בֶל mourning, funeral ceremony (24)

אֲבָל but, however, indeed, truly (11)

אָבַל (Q) to mourn, lament; (Hith) observe mourning rites (36)

אֶ֫בֶן (fs) stone; (fp) אֲבָנִים (276)

אִגֶּ֫רֶת letter, document; (fp) אִגְּרוֹת (10)

אָדוֹן lord, master; (of God 439x) אֲדֹנָי Lord (774)

אֹדוֹת because, on account of; (always with prep עַל) עַל אֹדוֹת (11)

אַדִּיר (adj) noble, majestic, mighty (27)

אָדַם (Q) to be red; (Pu) be reddened, dyed red (10)

אָדָם man, mankind, humankind (546)

אֲדָמָה ground, land, earth (222)

אֶ֫דֶן base, pedestal (57)

אַדֶּ֫רֶת cloak, robe (12)

אָהַב (Q) to love (of human and divine love); (Pi ptc) lover (217)

אַהֲבָה love (32)

אֲהָהּ ah! alas! (15)

אֹ֫הֶל tent (348)

אוֹ (conj) or (321)

אוֹב medium, necromancer, ghost (16)

אָוָה (Pi) to wish, desire, want; (Hith) crave, wish for, long for (30)

אוֹי woe! alas! (24)

אֱוִיל fool, idiot (26)

אוּלַי perhaps, maybe (45)

אוּלָם porch; also spelled אֵילָם (61)

אוּלָם but, however (19)

אִוֶּ֫לֶת folly, foolishness (25)

אָ֫וֶן iniquity, wickedness, evildoer (81)

אוֹן strength, vigor, manhood, wealth (16)

אוֹפַן wheel (35)

אוּץ (Q) to urge, press, be in a hurry, pressed (10)

אוֹצָר treasure, treasury, storehouse (79)

אוֹר (cs) light, daylight, sunshine (120)

אוֹר (Hi) to give light, shine, illuminate, light up (44)

אוֹת (cs) sign, mark, pledge; (cp) אֹתוֹת (79)

אָז then, since, before (141)

אֵזוֹב hyssop (10)

אֵזוֹר loincloth, girdle (14)

אֹ֫זֶן (fs) ear; (fd cstr) אָזְנֵי (188)

אָזַן (Hi) to give ear to, listen (to), hear, heed (41)

אָזַר (Q) to gird (on), equip (16)

אֶזְרָח native, citizen (17)

אָח brother; (ms cstr) אֲחִי; (mp) אַחִים (629)

אֶחָד one; (fs) אַחַת (976)

אָחוֹר back, behind (41)

אָחוֹת sister, relative, loved one (119)

אָחַז (Q) to seize, grasp, take hold (of), hold fast (63)

אֲחֻזָּה property, possession (66)

אָחַר (Pi) to delay, detain, hesitate, linger (18)

אַחֵר (adj) other, another; (fs) אַחֶ֫רֶת (166)

אַחֲרוֹן (adj) last, behind, west (51)

אַחֲרֵי (prep) after, behind; also spelled אַחַר (718)

אַחֲרִית end, extremity, last (61)

אֵי where? (33)

אִי coastland, island; (mp) אִיִּים (36)

אֹיֵב enemy (285)

אֵיד disaster, calamity (24)

אַיֵּה where? (52)

אֵיךְ how? (61)

אֵיכָה how? where? (17)

אַ֫יִל ram, ruler; (adj) mighty (171)

אַ֫יִל pillar, doorpost (22)

אַיָּל (male) deer, stag (11)

אַיָּלָה (female) deer, doe (11)

אֵימָה terror, fright, horror (17)

אַ֫יִן (particle of nonexistence) is not, are not, nothing; most often spelled אֵין (790)

אַ֫יִן wherefrom? whence? (17)

אֵיפָה a dry measurement of corn or wheat, ephah (40)

אֵיפֹה where? (10)

אִישׁ man, husband; (mp) אֲנָשִׁים (2,188)

אֵיתָן (adj) everflowing, constant, enduring; (mp) אֵתָנִים (14)

אַךְ only, surely, nevertheless (161)

אָכַל (Q) to eat, consume; (Ni) be eaten, consumed; (Hi) feed (820)

אֹ֫כֶל food (38)

אָכְלָה food, nourishment (18)

אָכֵן surely, truly, however (17)

אַל (neg particle) no, not (729)

אֶל־ (prep) to, toward, into; (with 3ms suff) אֵלָיו (5,518)

אֵל God, god (237)

אָלָה oath, curse (34)

אֵ֫לֶּה (cp dmstr pron and adj) these (744)

אֵלָה oak, terebinth, large tree (13)

אֱלֹהִים God, gods (2,602)

אֱלוֹהַּ God, god (58)

אֵלוֹן large (oak) tree (10)

אַלּוּף tribal chief, leader (60)

אֱלִיל worthlessness, idol (21)

אַלְמָנָה widow (55)

אֶ֫לֶף thousand; (md) אַלְפַּ֫יִם two thousand (496)

אֶ֫לֶף clan, tribe, region (11)

אֵם (fs) mother; (with 3ms suff) אִמּוֹ (220)

אִם if (1,070); כִּי־אִם but, except, only

אָמָה female slave or servant, maidservant (56)

אַמָּה cubit (distance between elbow and tip of middle finger), forearm (249)

אֱמוּנָה faithfulness, reliability (49)

אָמַל to dry up, waste away, languish (15)

אָמֵן amen, surely, truly (30)

אָמַן (Ni) to be reliable, faithful or trustworthy; (Hi) believe (in), trust, have trust in, put trust in (97)

אָמֵץ (Q) to be strong, be bold; (Pi) make firm, strengthen, harden someone's heart (41)

אָמַר (Q) to say; (Ni) be said, called; (Hi) declare, proclaim (5,316)

אֹ֫מֶר word, saying, speech (48)

אִמְרָה word, saying (36)

אֱמֶת truth, fidelity; (with 2ms suff) אֲמִתְּ֫ךָ (127)

אַמְתַּ֫חַת sack, bag (15)

אָנָּא please! I ask you!; also spelled אָנָּה (13)

אָ֫נָה where? עַד־אָנָה how long? also spelled אָן (42)

אֱנוֹשׁ man, humankind (42)

אָנַח (Ni) to sigh, groan (13)

אֲנָחָה sighing, groaning (11)

אֲנַ֫חְנוּ (1cp pers pron) we (121)

אֲנִי (1cs pers pron) I (874)

אֳנִיָּה ship, boat (32)

אָנֹכִי (1cs pers pron) I (359)

אָנַף (Q) to be angry (14)

אָסִיר prisoner (14)

אָסַף (Q) to gather (in), take in, take away, destroy; (Ni) be gathered, taken away, assemble (200)

אָסַר (Q) to tie, bind, fetter, imprison (73)

אִסָּר obligation, pledge, vow; also spelled אֱסָר (11)

אַף nostril, nose; (metaphorically) anger; (md) אַפַּ֫יִם (277)

אַף (conj) also, indeed, even (133)

אֵפֹד ephod, priestly garment (49)

אָפָה (Q) to bake (25)

אֵפוֹא then, so; also spelled אֵפוֹ (15)

אָפִיק river, channel, stream bed (18)

אֲפֵלָה darkness, gloominess (10)

אֶ֫פֶס end, nothing (43)

אֵ֫פֶר ashes, dust (22)

אֶצְבַּע (fs) finger, toe (31)

אֵ֫צֶל (prep) beside, near (62)

אָרַב (Q) to ambush, lie in ambush, lie in wait (41)

אַרְבֶּה (ms) locust (24)

אַרְבַּע four; (fs) אַרְבָּעָה; (mp) אַרְבָּעִים forty (455)

אָרַג (Q) to weave; (Q ptc) weaver (13)

אַרְגָּמָן purple (38)

אֲרוֹן (cs) ark, chest, coffin (202); אֲרוֹן הַבְּרִית "the ark of the covenant"

אֶ֫רֶז cedar (73)

אֹ֫רַח (cs) road, path, way (59)

אֲרִי lion; (mp) אֲרָיוֹת (35)

אַרְיֵה (ms) lion (47)

אָרַךְ (Hi) to make long, lengthen, extend (34)

אָרֵךְ (adj) long, slow (15); 13x אֶרֶךְ־אַפַּיִם (lit) "long of nose;" (idiom) slow to anger or patient

אֹ֫רֶךְ length (95)

אַרְמוֹן palace, stronghold (32)

אֶ֫רֶץ (fs) land, earth, ground (2,505)

אָרַר (Q) to curse (63)

אָרַשׂ (Pi) to betroth, be engaged; (Pu) be(come) betrothed or engaged (11)

אֵשׁ (cs) fire (376)

אִשָּׁה woman, wife; (fs cstr) אֵ֫שֶׁת; (fp) נָשִׁים (781)

אִשֶּׁה (ms) offering by fire (65)

אָשַׁם (Q) to be(come) guilty, commit an offense (35)

אָשָׁם guilt, guilt offering (46)

אַשְׁמָה guilt, blame (19)

אֲשֶׁר (rel pron) who, that, which (5,503)

אָשַׁר (Pi) to call or consider blessed, fortunate or happy; (Pu) be called blessed, fortunate or happy (10)

אֲשֵׁרָה Asherah (pagan goddess), cultic pole; (fp) אֲשֵׁרִים and אֲשֵׁרוֹת (40)

אַשְׁרֵי blessed, happy (44)

אַתְּ (2fs pers pron) you (67)

אֵת (definite direct object marker) not translated; also spelled אֶת־ with loss of accent or (with 3ms suff) אֹתוֹ (10,978)

אֵת (prep) with, beside; also spelled אֶת־ with loss of accent or (with 3ms suff) אִתּוֹ (890)

אָתָה (Q) to come; (Hi) bring (21)

אַתָּה (2ms pers pron) you (749)

אָתוֹן (fs) female donkey (34)

אַתֶּם (2mp pers pron) you (283)

אֶתְנַן wages, payment, gift (11)

ב

בְּ (prep) in, at, with, by, against (15,559)

בְּאֵר (fs) well, pit, cistern (37)

בָּאַשׁ (Q) to stink, have a bad smell; (Hi) make odious, become hated (18)

בָּגַד (Q) to act or deal treacherously, faithlessly or deceitfully with (49)

בֶּ֫גֶד clothes, garment, covering (216)

בִּגְלַל because of, on account of (10)

בַּד carrying pole, gate bar (40)

בַּד linen cloth (23)

בָּדָד alone, by oneself (11)

בָּדַל (Ni) to separate oneself, withdraw; (Hi) divide, separate, set apart, make a distinction (between), single out (42)

בֶּ֫דֶק damage, breach, crack (10)

בָּהַל (Ni) to be terrified, horrified, dismayed, disturbed, hasty, make haste; (Pi) terrify, make haste, act hastily (39)

בְּהֵמָה animal(s), beast(s), cattle (190)

בֹּ֫הֶן thumb, big toe (16)

בַּהֶ֫רֶת white spot on the skin (12)

בּוֹא (Q) to go in, enter, come to, come upon; (Hi) bring (in), come (in); (Hoph) be brought (2,592)

בּוּז (Q) to show contempt (for), despise (14)

בּוּז contempt (11)

בּוּס (Q) to tread down, trample under foot (12)

בּוֹר pit, cistern, well (67)

בּוֹשׁ (Q) to be ashamed; (Hi) put to shame (125)

בַּז plunder, spoil (25)

בָּזָה (Q) to despise, regard with contempt (42)

בִּזָּה spoil, plunder (10)

בָּזַז (Q) to plunder, spoil (43)

בָּחַן (Q) to test, put to the test, try, examine (29)

בָּחוּר young man; (mp) בַּחוּרִים (44)

בָּחִיר (adj) chosen, elect (13)

בָּחַר (Q) to choose, test, examine (172)

בָּטַח (Q) to trust, rely upon (118)

בֶּ֫טַח security, safety (42)

בֶּ֫טֶן (fs) belly, stomach, womb (72)

בִּי please, with your permission (12)

בֵּין (prep) between (409)

בִּין (Q) to understand, perceive, consider, give heed to; (Ni) be discerning, have understanding; (Hi) understand, teach; (Hith) show oneself perceptive (171)

בִּינָה understanding, insight (38)

בִּירָה citadel, fortress (18)

בַּ֫יִת (ms) house, household, (metaphorically) dynasty; (1497x ms cstr) בֵּית; (mp) בָּתִּים (2,047)

בָּכָה (Q) to weep (in grief or joy), weep (for) (114)

בְּכוֹר firstborn, oldest offspring (120)

בִּכּוּרִים firstfruits, early harvest (17)

בְּכִי weeping (30)

בְּכֹרָה birthright, right of the firstborn (12)

בַּל (poetic) no, never (73)

בָּלָה (Q) to be(come) worn out, used up or exhausted (16)

בַּלָּהָה sudden terror, horror (10)

בְּלִי without, nothing (59)

בְּלִיַּ֫עַל (adj) useless, worthless; (n) worthlessness (27)

בָּלַל (Q) to mix (up), confuse or confound (languages), mingle (44)

בָּלַע (Q, Pi) to swallow (up), engulf (42)

בִּלְעֲדֵי (prep) apart from, except for, without (17)

בִּלְתִּי (negates inf cstr) not, except; also spelled לְבִלְתִּי (86x) with prep לְ (112)

בָּמָה (cultic) high place, sacred hill; (fp) בָּמוֹת (106)

בְּמוֹ (prep) in, at, with, by, against; alternate (poetic) form of prep בְּ (10)

בֵּן son; (ms cstr) בֶּן־; (mp) בָּנִים; (mp cstr) בְּנֵי (4,941)

בָּנָה (Q) to build (up), rebuild, build (establish) a family; (Ni) be built, have a child (by or from) (377)

בַּעֲבוּר on account of, in order that (49)

בַּ֫עַד (prep) behind, through (104)

בָּעַל (Q) to rule over, be(come) lord or husband of, marry, own (take someone into possession as betrothed) (16)

בַּ֫עַל owner, master, husband, (divine title) Baal (161)

בָּעַר (Q) to burn (up), consume; (Pi) kindle, burn (60)

בָּעַר (Pi) to graze, sweep away, remove, get rid of, purge (27)

בָּעַת (Pi) to terrify, frighten, startle (16)

בָּצוּר (adj) fortified, inaccessible (26)

בָּצַע (Q) to cut off, sever, break off (away), make profit (16)

בֶּ֫צַע unjust gain or profit (23)

בָּקַע (Q) to cleave, split, breach, break open; (Ni) be cleft, split (open); (Pi) split, rip open (51)

בִּקְעָה valley, plain (19)

בָּקָר cattle, herd (183)

בֹּ֫קֶר morning (213)

בָּקַשׁ (Pi) to seek, search for, look for, discover, demand, require; (Pu) be sought (225)

בַּר grain, corn, wheat (14)

בָּרָא (Q) to create (only with God as subject); (Ni) be created (48)

בָּרָד hail (29)

בְּרוֹשׁ pine tree, juniper (20)

בַּרְזֶל iron (76)

בָּרַח (Q) to run away, flee, go or pass through (63)

בָּרִיא (adj) fat, well fed (14)

בְּרִיחַ bar (41)

בְּרִית covenant (287)

בֶּ֫רֶךְ (fs) knee (26)

בָּרַךְ (Q pass ptc) blessed, praised, adored; (Pi) bless, praise (327)

בְּרֵכָה pool, pond, reservoir (17)

בְּרָכָה blessing, gift (71)

בָּרָק lightning (21)

בָּרַר (Q) to purify, purge, sort, choose, select (16)

בֹּ֫שֶׂם spice, perfume (30)

בָּשַׂר (Pi) to bring good news, tell, announce (24)

בָּשָׂר flesh, meat, skin (270)

בָּשַׁל (Q) to boil; (Pi) boil, cook, roast (28)

בֹּ֫שֶׁת shame, disgrace (41)

בַּת daughter; (fp) בָּנוֹת (587)

בַּת (ms) liquid measurement, bath; (mp) בַּתִּים (13)

בְּתוֹךְ (prep) in the midst (middle) of, inside (319); combination of (prep) בְּ and (n) תָּוֶךְ (middle, center); also מִתּוֹךְ (68x) and אֶל־תּוֹךְ (22x)

בְּתוּלָה virgin (50)

בְּתוּלִים virginity, evidence of virginity (10)

ג

גַּאֲוָה pride, arrogance (19)

גָּאוֹן majesty, exaltation, pride (49)

גָּאַל (Q) to redeem, act as kinsman (perform the responsibilities of the next-of-kin), avenge (104)

גָּאַל (Ni, Pu) to be defiled, become impure; (Hith) defile oneself (11)

גְּאֻלָּה right of redemption, next-of-kin (14)

גַּב something curved, back, eyebrow, rim (of a wheel) (12)

גָּבַהּ (Q) to be high, tall, lofty, exalted or haughty; (Hi) make high, exalt (34)

גֹּבַהּ (ms) height, pride (17)

גָּבֹהַּ (adj) high, exalted; (fs) גְּבֹהָה (41)

גְּבוּל border, boundary, territory (251)

גִּבּוֹר (adj) mighty, valiant, heroic; (n) hero (160)

גְּבוּרָה power, strength; (fp) גְּבוּרוֹת mighty deeds (62)

גָּבִיעַ cup, bowl (14)

גְּבִירָה mistress, lady, queen mother (15)

גִּבְעָה hill (72)

גָּבַר (Q) to be strong, mighty, superior, excel, achieve, accomplish, prevail (25)

גֶּבֶר strong man, young man, hero (66)

גָּג roof; (mp) גַּגּוֹת (31)

גְּדוּד band of raiders, military troops (31)

גָּדוֹל (adj) great, big, large (527)

גְּדוּלָּה greatness, great deed (13)

גְּדִי young goat, kid (16)

גָּדַל (Q) to grow up, be(come) great, strong, wealthy, important; (Pi) bring up (children), make great, extol; (Hi) make great, magnify, do great things (117)

גֹּ֫דֶל greatness, arrogance (13)

גָּדַע (Q) to cut off, cut down; (Ni) be cut off, cut down, cut into pieces; (Pi) cut down, cut to pieces (22)

גָּדַר (Q) to build a wall, block a road (10)

גָּדֵר wall (of stone) (15)

גּוֹי nation, people; (mp) גּוֹיִם (567)

גְּוִיָּה body, corpse (13)

גּוֹלָה captivity, exiles (42)

גָּוַע (Q) to die, expire, pass away, perish (24)

גּוּר (Q) to sojourn, dwell (stay) as a foreigner or alien (82)

גּוּר (Q) to be afraid, dread, stand in awe (10)

גּוֹרָל lot, portion, allotment (77)

גָּזַז (Q) to shear, cut (15)

גָּזִית cut stone (11)

גָּזַל (Q) to tear off, tear away, seize, rob, take away by force (30)

גָּזַר (Q) to cut (in two, in pieces), divide, cut down, decide; (Ni) be cut off (from), decided (12)

גַּ֫חֶלֶת coal, burning charcoal (18)

גַּיְא (cs) valley; also spelled גֵּיא (64)

גִּיל (Q) to shout with joy, rejoice (47)

גַּל heap, pile; (mp) גַּלִּים (18)

גַּל wave (16)

גֻּלְגֹּלֶת head, skull (12)

גָּלָה (Q) to uncover, reveal, disclose; (Ni) uncover, reveal oneself, be revealed, exposed; (Pi) uncover, reveal, disclose; (Hi) take (carry away) into exile (187)

גֻּלָּה bowl, basin (15)

גִּלּוּלִים idols (48)

גָּלוּת exile, exiles (15)

גָּלַח (Pi) to shave (23)

גָּלַל (Q) to roll (away) (18)

גַּם also, even (769)

גְּמוּל recompense, requital (19)

גָּמַל (Q) to complete, finish, wean, ripen, render; recompense, requite (37)

גָּמָל camel; (mp) גְּמַלִּים (54)

גַּן (cs) garden; (cp) גַּנִּים (41)

גָּנַב (Q) to steal, deceive (40)

גַּנָּב thief, kidnapper (17)

גַּנָּה garden, orchard (12)

גָּעַל (Q) to loathe, abhor, feel disgust (10)

גָּעַר (Q) to rebuke, reproach (14)

גְּעָרָה rebuke, threat (15)

גָּעַשׁ (Q) to shake (10)

גֶּ֫פֶן (cs) vine, grapevine (55)

גֵּר stranger, sojourner, alien (92)

גָּרָה (Hith) to strive (against), oppose, battle (15)

גֵּרָה cud (11)

גֹּ֫רֶן (fs) threshing floor (37)

גָּרַע (Q) to shave, trim (a beard), diminish, restrain, withdraw (21)

גָּרַשׁ (Q) to drive out, banish; (Pi) drive out (away) (45)

גֶּ֫שֶׁם rain, showers (35)

ד

דֹּב bear (12)

דְּבִיר inner sanctuary, most holy place (16)

דָּבַק (Q) to cling, cleave to, stick to; (Hi) cause to cling, cleave or stick to, pursue closely (55)

דָּבָר word, matter, thing (1,454)

דָּבַר (Q) to speak (rare in Q); (Pi) speak (1,136)

דֶּ֫בֶר plague, pestilence (46)

דְּבַשׁ honey (54)

דָּג fish (19)

דָּגָה fish (15)

דֶּ֫גֶל division of a tribe, banner, standard (14)

דָּגָן grain, corn (40)

דּוֹד beloved, uncle (61)

דּוֹר generation; also spelled דֹּר; (mp) דֹּרוֹת and דֹּרֹת (167)

דּוּשׁ (Q) to tread on, trample down (out), thresh, exterminate, destroy; also spelled דִּישׁ (16)

דַּי what is required or necessary; (ms cstr) דֵּי (39)

דִּין (Q) to judge, minister or execute judgment, plead one's cause, contend with (24)

דִּין judgment, legal claim (19)

דָּכָא (Pi) to crush, beat to pieces (18)

דַּל (adj) poor, weak, needy (48)

דֶּלֶת door (88)

דָּם blood; bloodshed (361)

דָּמָה (Q) to be like, resemble; (Pi) liken, compare (30)

דָּמָה (Ni) to be destroyed, ruined (12)

דְּמוּת likeness, form, image (25)

דָּמַם (Q) to be silent, still, motionless, (struck) dumb, keep quiet, stand still (19)

דִּמְעָה (coll) tears (23)

דַּעַת knowledge, understanding, ability (88)

דַּק (adj) thin, lean, skinny; (fp) דַּקּוֹת (14)

דָּקַק (Q) to crush, become fine through grinding; (Hi) crush fine, pulverize; (Hoph) be crushed fine (12)

דָּקַר (Q) to pierce (through), run through; (Pu) be pierced through (11)

דָּרוֹם south, south wind (17)

דָּרַךְ (Q) to tread (often in the sense of pressing for wine or oil), march, draw a bow; (Hi) cause to tread, march or walk (63)

דֶּרֶךְ (cs) way, road, journey (712)

דָּרַשׁ (Q) to seek, inquire (of or about), investigate, require, demand (165)

דֶּשֶׁא grass, vegetation (14)

דָּשֵׁן (Pi) to refresh, revive, clean away fat ashes; (Pu) be made fat (11)

דֶּשֶׁן fat, fat-soaked ashes (15)

דָּת law, decree (22)

ה

הַ· (definite article) the (24,058)

הֲ (interrog particle) prefixed to the first word of a question (664)

הֶאָח aha! (12)

הֶ֫בֶל vanity, futility, breath (73)

הָגָה (Q) to utter a sound, growl, moan, groan, coo (of a dove), speak, proclaim (25)

הָדַף (Q) to thrust (away, out), push (away), drive away (out), shove (11)

הָדָר majesty, glory, splendor (30)

הוּא (3ms pers pron) he, it; (ms dmstr pron and adj) that (1,398)

הוֹד splendor, majesty (24)

הַוָּה destruction, ruin (13)

הוֹי woe! oh! ha! (51)

הוֹן wealth, possessions (26)

הִיא (3fs pers pron) she, it; (fs dmstr pron and adj) that; also spelled הִוא in the Pentateuch (491)

הָיָה (Q) to be, become, happen, occur; (Ni) be done, brought about, come to pass, occur (3,576)

הֵיכָל temple, palace (80)

הִין liquid measurement, hin (22)

הָלְאָה beyond, far away, out there (16)

הָלַךְ (Q) to go, walk, (metaphorically) behave; (Pi) go, walk; (Hith) walk about, move to and fro (1,554)

הָלַל (Pi) to praise, sing hallelujah; (Pu) be praised, praiseworthy; (Hith) boast (146)

הָלַל (Q) to be infatuated, deluded; (Hithpolel) be mad, act like a madman (15)

הֲלֹם here, to here (12)

הֵם (3mp pers pron) they; (mp dmstr) those; also spelled הֵ֫מָּה (565)

הָמָה (Q) to make (a) noise, make a sound, roar, growl, moan, groan, be boisterous (34)

הָמוֹן multitude, crowd, sound, roar (85)

הָמַם (Q) to make (a) noise, confuse, bring into motion and confusion (army), discomfit, disturb (13)

הֵן behold, if (107)

הִנֵּה behold, look; (with 1cs suff) הִנְנִי (1,061)

הֵ֫נָּה here (59)

הֵ֫נָּה (3fp pers pron) they; (fp dmstr pron and adj) those (29)

הָפַךְ (Q) to turn, overturn, overthrow, destroy; (Ni) be destroyed, turned into, changed (95)

הַר mountain, hill, hill country; (mp) הָרִים (558)

הָרַג (Q) to kill, slay (167)

הָרָה (Q) to conceive, be(come) pregnant (43)

הָרָה (fs adj) pregnant (15)

הָרַס (Q) to tear down, demolish, destroy, throw down, overthrow; (Ni) be ruined (43)

ו

וְ (conj) and, but, also, even, then (50,524)

וָו hook, nail, peg (13)

ז

זֹאת (fs dmstr pron and adj) this (605)

זָבַח (Q) to slaughter (for sacrifice), sacrifice; (Pi) offer sacrifice, sacrifice (134)

זֶ֫בַח sacrifice (162)

זֵד (adj) proud, insolent, presumptuous (13)

זָדוֹן arrogance, presumption (11)

זֹה (dmstr adj) this (11); alternate form of **זֹאת** (#79)

זֶה (ms dmstr pron and adj) this (1,178)

זָהָב gold (392)

זָהַר (Hi) to warn (about), admonish, caution (22)

זוּ (dmstr pron and adj) this; (rel pron) who, that, which (15)

זוּב (Q) to flow (away), suffer a discharge (42)

זוֹב discharge (of body fluid), hemorrhage (13)

זוּלָה except, only (16)

זוֹנָה prostitute, harlot (34)

זִיד (Q) to act insolently; (Hi) boil or cook, become hot (with anger), behave arrogantly (10)

זַ֫יִת olive tree, olive; (mp) **זֵיתִים** (38)

זַךְ (adj) pure, clean (11)

זָכַר (Q) to remember; (Ni) be remembered, thought of; (Hi) remind (235)

זֵ֫כֶר memory, remembrance (23)

זָכָר male, man (82)

זִכָּרוֹן memorial, remembrance (24)

זִמָּה evil plan, shameful behavior (29)

זָמַם (Q) to consider, think, ponder, devise, plan (evil), purpose (13)

זָמַר (Pi) to sing, praise, make music, play an instrument (45)

זָנָב tail (11)

זָנָה (Q) to commit fornication, be a harlot (prostitute), be unfaithful (60)

זְנוּנִים prostitution, fornication (12)

זָנַח (Q) to reject, spurn (19)

זָעַם (Q) to curse, scold, denounce (12)

זַ֫עַם anger, indignation, curse (22)

זָעַק (Q) to cry (out), call for help, summon (73)

זְעָקָה outcry, call for help (19)

זָקֵן (adj) old; (n) elder, old man (180)

זָקֵן (Q) to be(come) old, grow old (26)

זָקָן (cs) beard (19)

זֵר frame, border, molding (10)

זָר (adj) foreign, strange (70)

זָרָה (Q) to scatter; (Pi) scatter, disperse, spread (38)

זְרוֹעַ (fs) arm, forearm; (metaphorically) strength or power; (fp) זְרֹעוֹת (91)

זָרַח (Q) to rise (sun), shine, come out, appear, break out (leprosy) (18)

זָרַע (Q) to sow, scatter seed (56)

זֶ֫רַע seed, offspring, descendants (229)

זָרַק (Q) to toss, throw, scatter, sprinkle (34)

ח

חָבָא (Ni) to hide (oneself), be hidden; (Hith) keep oneself hidden (34)

חָבַל (Q) to take, hold or seize (something) in pledge, exact a pledge from someone, bind by taking a pledge (13)

חָבַל (Q) to act corruptly or ruinously; (Pi) ruin, destroy (11)

חֶ֫בֶל rope, cord, field, region (48)

חָבַק (Q) to embrace, fold the hands (in idleness); (Pi) embrace (13)

חָבֵר associate, companion, friend (15)

חָבַר (Q) to unite, ally oneself (with), join forces (28)

חָבַשׁ (Q) to saddle, bind or buckle on, bind up (wound), wrap, twist (rope), imprison (33)

חַג feast, festival, procession; also spelled חָג; (mp) חַגִּים (62)

חָגַג (Q) to stagger, reel, celebrate a pilgrimage festival (16)

חָגַר (Q) to gird, gird (oneself or someone), get ready (44)

חָדַל (Q) to cease, end, stop, refrain (from) (55)

חֶ֫דֶר room, chamber (38)

חָדַשׁ (Pi) to make new, renew, restore (10)

חָדָשׁ (adj) new, fresh (53)

חֹ֫דֶשׁ month, new moon (283)

חָוָה (Hishtaphel) to bow down, worship (173)

חוֹחַ thorn, thornbush (11)

חוּל (Q) to go around, whirl (about), dance, writhe; also spelled חִיל (10)

חוֹל sand (22)

חוֹמָה wall (133)

חוּס (Q) to pity, look upon with compassion, spare (24)

חוּץ outside, street; (mp) חוּצוֹת; (prefixed with prep מִן) מִחוּץ from outside, outside (164)

חוּשׁ (Q) to hurry, make haste (18)

חוֹתָם seal, signet ring (14)

חָזָה (Q) to see, behold, perceive (55)

חֹזֶה (ms) seer (16)

חָזֶה (ms) breast (of sacrificial animal) (13)

חָזוֹן vision, revelation (35)

חָזַק (Q) to be(come) strong, have courage; (Pi) make strong, strengthen; (Hi) strengthen, seize, grasp, take hold of; (Hith) strengthen oneself, show oneself as strong or courageous (290)

חָזָק (adj) strong, mighty, hard (57)

חָטָא (Q) to miss (a goal or mark), sin, commit a sin; (Pi) make a sin offering; (Hi) cause to sin (240)

חֵטְא sin (34)

חַטָּא (adj) sinful; (n) sinner (19)

חַטָּאת sin, sin offering; (fs cstr) חַטַּאת; (fp cstr) חַטֹּאוֹת and חַטֹּאת (298)

חִטָּה wheat; (fp) חִטִּים (30)

חַי (adj) living, alive; (mp) חַיִּים (254)

חִידָה riddle, difficult or enigmatic question (17)

חָיָה (Q) to live, be alive, revive, restore to life; (Pi) preserve alive, let live, give life; (Hi) preserve, keep alive, revive, restore to life (283)

חַיָּה animal, beast, living thing (96)

חַיָּה life; (with 3ms suff) חַיָּתוֹ (11)

חַיִּים life, lifetime (140)

חִיל (Q) to writhe, travail, be in labor, tremble; also spelled חוּל (48)

חַ֫יִל strength, wealth, army (246)

חִיצוֹן (adj) outer, external (25)

חֵיק bosom, lap (38)

חֵךְ roof of the mouth, palate (18)

חָכָה (Pi) to wait (for), tarry, long for, be patient (14)

חָכַם (Q) to be(come) wise, act wisely (28)

חָכָם (adj) wise, skillful, experienced (138)

חָכְמָה wisdom, skill (153)

חָלָב milk (44)

חֵ֫לֶב fat; (metaphorically) best, choice part (92)

חָלָה (Q) to be(come) weak, tired, sick; (Ni) be exhausted; (Pi) appease, flatter (75)

חַלָּה cake, ring-shaped bread (14)

חֲלוֹם dream (65)

חַלּוֹן (cs) window; (cp) חַלּוֹנוֹת and חַלּוֹנִים (32)

חֳלִי illness, sickness (24)

חָלִיל far be it! never! (21); חָלִ֫ילָה לִּי "far be it from me!"

חֲלִיפָה change, shift, relief; (fp) חֲלִיפוֹת (12)

חָלָל (adj) pierced, slain, defiled (94)

חָלַל (Ni) to be defiled, profaned, defile oneself; (Pi) profane, pollute, defile; (Hi) let something be profaned (135)

חָלַם (Q) to dream (29)

חָלַף (Q) to pass on or away (quickly), pass by, vanish; (Hi) change, replace, substitute (26)

חָלַץ (Q) to draw out, take off, withdraw, be girded (ready for battle); (Pi) rescue, deliver (44)

חֲלָצַ֫יִם (md) loins, stomach, waist (11)

חָלַק (Q) to divide, share (with or in), apportion, distribute; (Pi) divide (in pieces), apportion, scatter (55)

חָלָק (adj) smooth, slippery, flattering (10)

חֵ֫לֶק portion, share (66)

חֶלְקָה piece (of land), portion (23)

חֹם heat, warmth (10)

חֶמְאָה butter, cream, curdled milk (10)

חָמַד (Q) to desire, take pleasure (delight) in, crave, covet (21)

חֶמְדָּה something desirable, precious or valuable (16)

חֵמָה wrath, heat, poison (125)

חֲמוֹר donkey (96)

חָמוֹת mother-in-law (11)

חֲמִישִׁי (adj) fifth; (fs) חֲמִישִׁית (45)

חָמַל (Q) to have compassion (for), have pity (for), spare (41)

חָמַם (Q) to be(come) warm (23)

חָמָס violence, wrong (60)

חָמֵץ leaven, something leavened (11)

חֹמֶר mud, clay, mortar (17)

חֹמֶר dry measurement, heap, pile, homer (13)

חָמֵשׁ five; (fs) חֲמִשָּׁה; (mp) חֲמִשִּׁים fifty (508)

חֵן favor, grace, charm (69)

חָנָה (Q) to decline, camp, encamp, pitch camp, lay siege to (143)

חַנּוּן (adj) gracious, merciful (13)

חֲנִית spear (48)

חִנָּם without cause, without compensation, for nothing or in vain (32)

חָנַן (Q) to be gracious to, show favor to, favor; (Hith) plead for grace, favor or compassion (77)

חָנֵף (Q) to be godless (of a priest or prophet), defiled (of land); (Hi) defile, pollute (11)

חָנֵף (adj) godless, profane (13)

חֶ֫סֶד loyalty, faithfulness, steadfast love, lovingkindness (249)

חָסָה (Q) to seek or take refuge (37)

חָסִיד (adj) godly, faithful, pious (34)

חָסֵר (Q) to diminish, decrease, lack (22)

חָסֵר (adj) lacking, wanting; (ms cstr) חֲסַר (17)

חָפָה (Q) to cover; (Pi) overlay (with) (12)

חָפַז (Q) to be in a hurry, hurry away (in alarm or fear), hasten in alarm; (Ni) run away in alarm (10)

חָפֵץ (Q) to delight in, take pleasure in, desire, be willing (74)

חָפֵץ delighting (in), desiring (13)

חֵ֫פֶץ delight, desire, pleasure, joy (38)

חָפַר (Q) to dig, track, search (for), scout out, spy out (23)

חָפֵר (Q) to be ashamed (17)

חָפַשׂ (Q) to search (out), examine; (Pi) search thoroughly, track down; (Hith) disguise oneself (23)

חָפְשִׁי (adj) free, exempt (17)

חֵץ arrow; (mp) חִצִּים (55)

חָצַב (Q) to quarry, hew (out), dig, dress (stones) (16)

חָצָה (Q) to divide (into) (15)

חֲצִי half, middle (125)

חָצִיר grass (17)

חֲצֹצְרָה trumpet (29)

חָצֵר (cs) courtyard, village, settlement; (cp) חֲצֵרִים and חֲצֵרוֹת (192)

חֹק statute, appointed time, portion; (mp) חֻקִּים (131)

חֻקָּה statute, ordinance (104)

חָקַק (Q) to hew out or carve out (a grave), inscribe, engrave, enact, decree (19)

חָקַר (Q) to explore, search, spy out (27)

חֵ֫קֶר searching, something searched out (12)

חֹר noble, free person (13)

חָרֵב (Q) to dry up (intransitive), lie in ruins; (Hi) cause to dry up, lay waste, make desolate (36)

חָרֵב (adj) dry, desolate, wasted (10)

חֹ֫רֶב dryness, drought, heat, waste (16)

חֶ֫רֶב (fs) sword (413)

חָרְבָּה desolation, ruin; (fp) חֳרָבוֹת (42)

חָרַד (Q) to tremble, do something with trembling, shudder, quake; (Hi) startle (39)

חָרָה (Q) to be(come) hot, burn with anger, become angry (93)

חָרוֹן anger, fury, burning (41)

חַרְטֹם magician, soothsayer priest; (mp) חַרְטֻמִּים (11)

חָרַם (Hi) to devote to the ban, dedicate to destruction, exterminate (50)

חֵ֫רֶם something set apart for destruction, devoted to destruction (29)

חָרַף (Q) to taunt, reproach; (Pi) taunt, reproach, revile (38)

חֶרְפָּה reproach, disgrace, shame (73)

חָרַץ (Q) to decide, cut (10)

חֶ֫רֶשׂ earthenware, potsherd (20)

חָרָשׁ craftsman (36)

חָרַשׁ (Q) to be silent, deaf; (Hi) be(come) silent, deaf, keep still (47)

חָרַשׁ (Q) to plow, engrave, devise, plan (27)

חָשַׂךְ (Q) to withhold, keep back, refrain, spare, save, restrain (28)

חָשַׂף (Q) to strip, strip off, bare, skim or scoop off (10)

חָשַׁב (Q) to think, consider, devise, plan, value, reckon; (Ni) be reckoned, accounted, considered (as); (Pi) think, consider, devise, plan (124)

חָשָׁה (Q) to be silent; (Hi) be silent, order (someone) to be silent, hesitate, delay (16)

חָשַׁךְ (Q) to be(come) dark, grow dim (eyes) (17)

חֹשֶׁךְ darkness (80)

חֹשֶׁן breastplate (of the high priest) (25)

חָשַׁק (Q) to be attached to, cling to, love (11)

חָתַם (Q) to seal (up), affix a seal (27)

חָתַן (Hith) to intermarry with, become related by marriage, become a son-in-law (11)

חָתָן bridegroom, son-in-law (20)

חֹתֵן father-in-law (21)

חָתַת (Q) to be shattered, dismayed, filled with terror (55)

ט

טָבַח (Q) to slaughter, butcher, slay (11)

טַבָּח guard, cook (32)

טֶבַח slaughtering, slaughter (12)

טָבַל (Q) to dip (something into) (16)

טָבַע (Q) to sink, penetrate; (Hoph) be sunk, settled, or planted (10)

טַבַּעַת ring, signet ring; (fp) טַבָּעֹת (50)

טָהוֹר (adj) clean, pure (96)

טָהֵר (Q) to be clean (ceremonially), pure (morally); (Pi) cleanse, purify, pronounce clean; (Hith) purify or cleanse oneself (94)

טָהֳרָה purification, purity, ceremonial cleanness (13)

טוֹב (adj) good, pleasant (530)

טוֹב (Q) to be good, pleasing, pleasant, joyful, well with (44)

טוּב goodness, well-being, happiness (32)

טוּחַ (Q) to plaster (wall of a house), coat, overlay (11)

טוּל (Hi) to throw (far), cast, hurl; (Hoph) be thrown, hurled (14)

טוּר row, course (of stones) (26)

טִיט mud, mire, clay (13)

טַל dew, light rain (31)

טָמֵא (Q) to be(come) unclean; (Ni) defile oneself; (Pi) defile, pronounce or declare unclean; (Hith) defile oneself, become unclean (162)

טָמֵא (adj) unclean (88)

טֻמְאָה uncleanness, impurity (36)

טָמַן (Q) to hide (31)

טָעַם (Q) to taste, eat, savor food (11)

טַ֫עַם taste, sense, discernment (13)

טַף children (41)

טֶ֫רֶם before, not yet; also spelled בְּטֶרֶם with prep בְּ (56)

טָרַף (Q) to tear (in pieces), rend (25)

טֶ֫רֶף prey, food (22)

י

יָאַל (Hi) to be intent on something, be determined, show willingness or undertake to do something (18)

יְאֹר stream, river, Nile (64)

יְבוּל produce, harvest, crop (13)

יָבַל (Hi) to bring (as gift or tribute), lead; (Hoph) be brought, led (18)

יָבֵשׁ (Q) to dry up, be(come) dry, wither; (Hi) make dry (up), make wither (59)

יַבָּשָׁה dry land, dry ground (14)

יָגוֹן grief, sorrow, agony (14)

יְגִיעַ labor, work, product of labor, gain (16)

יָגַע (Q) to toil, labor, struggle, grow or be weary (26)

יָד (fs) hand; (metaphorically) power (1,627)

יָדָה (Hi) to thank, praise, confess; (Hith) confess (111)

יָדַע (Q) to know, know sexually (have intercourse with); (Ni) be(come) known, reveal oneself; (Hi) make known, inform (956)

יִדְּעֹנִי soothsayer (11)

יָהַב (Q) to givc, come (33)

יוֹבֵל ram's horn, trumpet, (year of) jubilee (27)

יוֹם day; (mp) **יָמִים** (2,301)

יוֹמָם by day, daily, in the daytime (53)

יוֹנָה dove; (fp) **יוֹנִים** (33)

יַחַד together, along with (46)

יַחְדָּו together, at the same time (96)

יָחִיד (adj) only (child), lonely, solitary (12)

יָחַל (Pi, Hi) to wait (for), hope for (42)

יָחַשׂ (Hith) to be registered or enrolled in a genealogical list; (Hith inf as noun) genealogy, registration (20)

יָטַב (Q) to be well with, go well with, be pleasing (to); (Hi) make things go well for, do good to, deal well with, treat kindly (117)

יַ֫יִן wine; (ms cstr) יֵין (141)

יָכַח (Hi) to reprove, rebuke, reproach, chasten, punish, decide, mediate, arbitrate (59)

יָכֹל (Q) to be able, capable of, endure, prevail (193)

יָלַד (Q) to bear (children), give birth, bring forth, beget; (Ni) be born; (Pi) help at birth, serve as midwife; (Pu) be born; (Hi) become the father of, beget (499)

יֶ֫לֶד child, boy, youth (89)

יָלִיד (adj) born (of); (n) son, slave (13)

יָלַל (Hi) to howl, lament, wail (31)

יָם sea; (mp) יַמִּים (396)

יָמִין (fs) right hand, south (141)

יְמָנִית (fs adj) right, southern; (ms) יְמָנִי (33)

יָנָה (Q, Hi) to oppress, mistreat (19)

יָנַק (Q) to suck; (Hi) suckle, nurse (33)

יָסַד (Q) to found, establish, appoint, destine, allocate; (Pi) found, appoint, establish (41)

יְסוֹד foundation wall, base (20)

יָסַף (Q) to add, continue (to do something again); (Hi) add, increase, do again and again (213)

יָסַר (Pi) to teach, discipline, correct, chastise, rebuke (41)

יָעַד (Q) to designate, appoint; (Ni) meet, gather or assemble by appointment (29)

יָעַל (Hi) to profit, gain profit, benefit (23)

יַ֫עַן on account of, because; 33x with אֲשֶׁר (#9) as יַ֫עַן אֲשֶׁר (100)

יָעַץ (Q) to advise, counsel, plan, decide; (Ni) consult or take counsel together (80)

יַ֫עַר forest, woods, thicket (57)

יָפֶה (adj) beautiful; (fs) יָפָה (42)

יֳפִי beauty (19)

יָצָא (Q) to go or come out; (Hi) cause to go or come out, lead out, bring out (1,076)

יָצַב (Hith) to take one's stand, stand firm, station oneself, present oneself before (48)

יָצַג (Hi) to set, place, establish, take one's stand (17)

יִצְהָר olive oil (23)

יָצַק (Q) to pour, pour out (liquid), cast (metal), flow (into); (Hoph) be cast, poured out, emptied out (53)

יָצַר (Q) to form, fashion, shape, create (63)

יָצַת (Q) to kindle, burn; (Hi) set on fire, set fire to (27)

יֶ֫קֶב wine vat, winepress (16)

יָקַץ (Q) to awake, wake up, become active (11)

יָקַר (Q) to be difficult, precious, prized, highly valued, esteemed, honored, costly or rare (11)

יְקָר precious thing, something valuable, honor, respect (17)

יָקָר (adj) precious, valuable (36)

יָרֵא (Q) to fear, be afraid, in awe of, reverence; (Ni) be feared, held in honor (317)

יָרֵא (adj) fearful (63)

יִרְאָה fear; (fs cstr) יִרְאַת (44); יִרְאַת יְהוָה "the fear of Yahweh"

יָרַד (Q) to go down, descend; (Hi) bring down, lead down (382)

יָרָה (Hi) to instruct, teach (47)

יָרָה (Q, Hi) to throw, shoot, cast (lots) (28)

יָרֵחַ moon (27)

יֶ֫רַח month (12)

יְרִיעָה tent curtain (54)

יָרֵךְ (fs) thigh, loin, side (34)

יְרֵכָה side, hip, far part, remote part (30)

יָרַשׁ (Q) to inherit, take possession of, dispossess, impoverish; (Hi) cause to possess or inherit, dispossess (232)

יְרֵשָּׁה possession, inheritance (14)

יֵשׁ (particle of existence) there is, there are (138)

יָשַׁב (Q) to sit (down), dwell, inhabit; (Hi) cause to sit or dwell, settle (a city) (1,088)

יְשׁוּעָה salvation, help, deliverance (78)

יְשִׁימוֹן desert, wilderness, wasteland (13)

יָשַׁן (Q) to sleep, go to sleep, be asleep (16)

יָשַׁע (Ni) to be delivered, victorious, receive help; (Hi) help, save, deliver, rescue, come to the aid of (205)

יֵ֫שַׁע salvation, deliverance, help; (with 1cs suff) יִשְׁעִי (36)

יָשַׁר (Q) to be straight, upright or right, please (27)

יָשָׁר (adj) upright, just (119)

יֹ֫שֶׁר uprightness, honesty, straightness (14)

יָתֵד (fs) tent peg, stake, pin (24)

יָתוֹם orphan (42)

יָתַר (Ni) to be left over, remain; (Hi) have (something) left over or remaining (106)

יֶ֫תֶר rest, remainder, excess (97)

יִתְרוֹן advantage, profit (10)

יֹתֶ֫רֶת covering, lobe (of an animal's liver) (11)

כ

כְּ (prep) as, like, according to; (with 2ms suff) כָּמ֫וֹךָ (3,053)

כָּבֵד (Q) to be heavy, weighty, honored; (Ni) be honored; (Pi) honor; (Hi) make heavy, dull or insensitive, harden (heart) (114)

כָּבֵד (adj) heavy, severe, important (41)

כָּבֵד (fs) liver (14)

כָּבָה (Q) to go out, be quenched, extinguished; (Pi) put out, quench, extinguish (24)

כָּבוֹד glory, splendor, honor, abundance (200); כְּבוֹד יְהוָה "the glory of Yahweh"

כַּבִּיר (adj) mighty, strong, powerful (10)

כָּבַס (Pi) to clean, cleanse, wash away guilt (51)

כֶּ֫בֶשׂ lamb, sheep (107)

כָּבַשׁ (Q) to subdue, subjugate, make subservient, bring into bondage, violate (rape) a woman; (Ni) be subdued, be subjugated (15)

כַּד (fs) jar, pitcher; (fp) כַּדִּים (18)

כֹּה thus, here (577)

כָּהַן (Pi) to perform the duties of a priest, minister as a priest (23)

כֹּהֵן priest; (mp) כֹּהֲנִים (750)

כְּהֻנָּה priesthood (14)

כּוֹכָב star (37)

כּוּל (Q) to comprehend; (Pilpel) contain, sustain, provide, support; (Hi) contain, hold (in), sustain, endure (38)

כּוּן (Ni) to be established, steadfast, ready, arranged, stand firm; (Hi) establish, set up, prepare, make ready, make firm; (Polel) set up, establish (219)

כּוֹס (fs) cup (31)

כָּזַב (Pi) to lie, deceive (16)

כָּזָב lie, deception, falsehood (31)

כֹּחַ strength, power (126)

כָּחַד (Ni) to be hidden, effaced; (Pi) hide, conceal (32)

כָּחַשׁ (Pi) to deny, delude, deceive, lie, act deceptively, feign submission or obedience (22)

כִּי that, because; (adversative) but, except; (emphatic) indeed, truly (4,487); כִּי־אִם but, except

כִּיּוֹר wash basin, cooking pot (23)

כָּכָה thus, so (37)

כִּכָּר (fs) something round, talent (weight), valley; (fp) כִּכָּרִים (68)

כֹּל all, each, every; (cstr) כָּל־ (5,415)

כָּלָא (Q) to shut up, restrain, withhold, keep back (17)

כֶּלֶא prison, confinement (10)

כֶּלֶב dog, male temple prostitute (32)

כָּלָה (Q) to be complete, finished, at an end, accomplished, spent, exhausted, come to an end; (Pi) complete, finish, bring to an end (207)

כָּלָה complete destruction, annihilation (22)

כַּלָּה daughter-in-law, bride (34)

כְּלִי vessel, implement, weapon; (mp) כֵּלִים; (mp cstr) כְּלֵי (325)

כְּלָיוֹת (fp) kidneys, place of thought or emotion (31)

כָּלִיל (adj) entire, whole, complete (15)

כָּלַם (Ni) to be hurt, humiliated, ashamed, disgraced; (Hi) put to shame, humiliate, disgrace (38)

כְּלִמָּה insult, disgrace, humiliation (30)

כֵּן so, thus (741)

כֵּן (adj) honest, correct, right (24)

כֵּן base, stand; (with 3ms suff) כַּנּוֹ (11)

כִּנּוֹר lyre, harp; (mp) כִּנֹּרוֹת (42)

כָּנַס (Q) to gather, collect, amass; (Pi) gather, assemble (11)

כָּנַע (Ni) to be subdued, humbled, humble oneself; (Hi) humble or subdue someone (36)

כָּנָף (fs) wing, edge, extremity (111)

כִּסֵּא seat, chair, throne (135)

כָּסָה (Q) to cover, conceal, hide; (Pi) cover (up), conceal, clothe (153)

כְּסִיל fool, shameless person (70)

כֶּ֫סֶף silver, money (403)

כָּעַס (Q) to be angry, vexed; (Hi) vex, provoke, provoke (God) to anger (55)

כַּ֫עַס anger, vexation (21)

כַּף (fs) hand, palm, sole of the foot (195)

כְּפִיר young lion (31)

כָּפַר (Pi) to cover (over), atone (for), make atonement (102)

כֹּ֫פֶר ransom, bribe (13)

כַּפֹּ֫רֶת mercy seat, place of atonement, lid (27)

כַּפְתֹּר decorative knob of a lampstand (18)

כַּר ram, battering ram; (mp) כָּרִים (12)

כָּרָה (Q) to dig, excavate, hollow out (14)

כְּרוּב cherub; (mp) כְּרוּבִים cherubim (91)

כֶּ֫רֶם vineyard (94)

כַּרְמֶל fertile field, orchard, plantation (15)

כָּרַע (Q) to bow (down), kneel (down), fall to one's knees (36)

כָּרַת (Q) to cut, cut off, cut down; (idiom) to make a covenant (with בְּרִית); (Ni) be cut off (down); (Hi) cut off, destroy, exterminate (289)

כֶּ֫שֶׂב young ram, lamb (13)

כָּשַׁל (Q) to stumble, totter, stagger; (Ni) be caused to stumble, stumble (65)

כָּתַב (Q) to write (upon), register, record; (Ni) be written (225)

כְּתָב writing, document, register (17)

כֻּתֹּ֫נֶת tunic, garment, robe; also spelled כְּתֹ֫נֶת (29)

כָּתֵף (fs) side, shoulder (67)

כֹּתֶ֫רֶת capital (top) of a pillar (24)

כָּתַת (Q) to beat, crush fine, hammer (into pieces); (Pi) beat, hammer, crush to pieces (17)

ל

לְ (prep) to, toward, for (20,321)

לֹא (neg particle) no, not; also spelled לוֹא (5,189)

לָאָה (Q) to be(come) tired or weary; (Ni) tire (oneself) out, be tired of something; (Hi) make weary (19)

לְאֹם people, nation; (mp) לְאֻמִּים (31)

לֵב heart, mind, will; (mp) לִבּוֹת; also spelled לֵבָב (854)

לְבַד alone, by oneself; (with 3ms suff) לְבַדּוֹ (161)

לְבוֹנָה frankincense (21)

לְבוּשׁ clothing, garment (32)

לָבִיא (cs) lion, lioness (12)

לָבָן (adj) white (29)

לְבֵנָה brick, tile, paving-stone; (fp) לְבֵנִים (12)

לָבַשׁ (Q) to put on a garment, clothe, be clothed; (Hi) clothe (112)

לַהַב flame, blade (of a sword) (12)

לֶהָבָה flame (19)

לָהַט (Q) to blaze, burn; (Pi) set ablaze, devour (with fire), scorch (10)

לוּ if only, oh that (23)

לָוָה (Q) to borrow; (Hi) lend to (14)

לָוָה (Ni) to join oneself to (12)

לוּחַ tablet, board, plank (43)

לוּלֵי if not, unless, except; also spelled לוּלֵא (14)

לוּן (Ni, Hi) to murmur (against), grumble (17)

לְחִי (fs) jaw, cheek, chin (21)

לֶחֶם bread, food (340)

לָחַם (Q, Ni) to fight, do battle with (rare in Q) (171)

לָחַץ (Q) to squeeze, crowd, press, oppress, torment (19)

לַחַץ oppression, affliction (12)

לַיְלָה (ms) night; (mp) לֵילוֹת (234)

לִין (Q) to remain overnight, spend the night (71)

לִיץ	(Q) to boast (28)
לָכַד	(Q) to take, capture, catch, seize; (Ni) be caught, captured (121)
לֻלָאֹת	(fp) loops, knots (13)
לָמַד	(Q) to learn; (Pi) teach (87)
לָ֫מָּה	why? also spelled לָמָה (178)
לְמַ֫עַן	(prep) on account of, for the sake of (272)
לָעַג	(Q, Hi) to mock, ridicule, deride (18)
לְעֻמַּת	(prep) beside, alongside, corresponding to; combination of prep לְ and עֻמָּה (32)
לַפִּיד	torch, lightning (14)
לָקַח	(Q) to take, grasp, capture, seize; (Ni) be captured, taken away (967)
לָקַט	(Q) to gather (together), glean; (Pi) gather (up), collect (37)
לָשׁוֹן	(cs) tongue, language (117)
לִשְׁכָּה	room, chamber, hall (48)

מ

מְאֹד	very, exceedingly (300)
מֵאָה	hundred; (fp) מֵאוֹת; (fd) מָאתַ֫יִם two hundred (583)
מְאוּמָה	(ms) something, anything (32)
מָאוֹר	light, luminary, light-bearer (18)
מֹאזְנַ֫יִם	balances, scales (15)
מַאֲכָל	food (30)
מָאֵן	(Pi) to refuse (41)
מָאַס	(Q) to refuse, reject, despise (74)
מָבוֹא	entrance, setting (of the sun), west (26)
מַבּוּל	flood, deluge (13)

מִבְחָר choicest, finest, best (people or things) (12)

מִבְטָח confidence, trust, security (15)

מִבְצָר fortress, stronghold (37)

מִגְדָּל tower; (mp) מִגְדָּלִים and מִגְדָּלוֹת (45)

מָגוֹר place of residence, temporary dwelling; (mp cstr) מְגוּרֵי (11)

מְגִלָּה scroll (21)

מָגֵן (cs) shield; (cp) מָגִנִּים (60)

מַגֵּפָה plague, slaughter (26)

מִגְרָשׁ open land, pasture (114)

מַד garment, clothes (11)

מִדְבָּר wilderness, desert, pasture (269)

מָדַד (Q) to measure, measure off (distance or expanse), measure out (grain) (52)

מִדָּה measure, measurement (55)

מָדוֹן strife, dispute, quarrel (17)

מַדּוּעַ why? (72)

מִדְיָן contention, quarrel (10)

מְדִינָה province, district (53)

מָה (interrog pron) what? also spelled מַה and מֶה (571)

מְהוּמָה confusion, dismay, panic (12)

מָהַר (Pi) to hasten, hurry, go or come quickly (81)

מְהֵרָה quickly, at once (20)

מוּג (Q) to waver, melt; (Ni) wave, sway back and forth, undulate (17)

מוֹט (Q) to totter, shake, sway, stagger; (Ni) be made to stagger, stumble or totter (39)

מוֹטָה yoke, bar, carrying pole (12)

מוּל (prep) in front of, opposite (36)

מוּל (Q) to circumcise; (Ni) be circumcised (32)

מוֹלֶ֫דֶת relatives, offspring, descendants (22)

מוּם defect, blemish (21)

מוּסָר discipline, correction, instruction (50)

מוֹעֵד appointed time (of feast), meeting place, assembly (223)

מוֹפֵת wonder, sign, miracle (36)

מוֹצָא act of going forth, exit, source, spring (27)

מוֹקֵשׁ snare, trap (27)

מוּר (Hi) to change, alter, exchange (14)

מוֹרָא fear, terror (11)

מוּשׁ (Q) to withdraw (from a place), cease from, leave off, depart (21)

מוֹשָׁב dwelling, settlement, seat; (mp) מוֹשָׁבוֹת (44)

מוּת (Q) to die; (Hi) kill, put to death; (Hoph) be killed (845)

מָ֫וֶת death, dying; (ms cstr) מוֹת (153)

מִזְבֵּחַ altar; (mp) מִזְבְּחוֹת (403)

מְזוּזָה doorpost, doorframe (19)

מְזִמָּה purpose, plan, deliberation (19)

מִזְמוֹר psalm, song (57)

מִזְרָח east, sunrise (74)

מִזְרָק bowl; (mp) מִזְרָקוֹת (32)

מָחָה (Q) to wipe (out), destroy, annihilate (34)

מְחִיר price, payment, money (15)

מַחֲ֫לֹקֶת division, portion (42)

מַחְמָד something desirable, precious thing (13)

מַחֲנֶה (cs) camp, army; (cp) מַחֲנוֹת and מַחֲנִים (215)

מַחְסֶה (ms) refuge, shelter (20)

מַחְסוֹר need, lack, poverty (13)

מָחַץ (Q) to smash, shatter, beat to pieces, smite (14)

מַחֲצִית half, middle (16)

מָחָר tomorrow (52)

מָחֳרָת (the) next day (32)

מַחֲשָׁבָה thought, plan, scheme (56)

מַחְתָּה fire pan, censer (22)

מְחִתָּה terror, ruin, destruction (11)

מַ֫טָּה downward, beneath, below (19)

מַטֶּה (ms) staff, rod, tribe; (mp) מַטּוֹת (252)

מִטָּה couch, bed (29)

מָטַר (Hi) to cause rain to fall, send rain (17)

מָטָר rain (38)

מַטָּרָה guard, prison, (archery) target (16)

מִי (interrog pron) who? (424)

מַ֫יִם water; (md cstr) מֵי (585)

מִין kind, type, species (31)

מִישׁוֹר plain, level ground, fairness (23)

מֵישָׁרִים level path, uprightness, fairness (19)

מַכְאוֹב pain, suffering (16)

מַכָּה wound, injury, defeat (48)

מָכוֹן place, site, foundation, support (17)

מְכוֹנָה stand, base, support (25)

מִכְסֶה (ms) cover, covering (16)

מָכַר (Q) to sell, hand over; (Ni) be sold, sell oneself (into slavery) (80)

מִכְשׁוֹל stumbling block, obstacle, offense (14)

מָלֵא (Q) to be full, fill (up); (Ni) be filled (with); (Pi) fill, perform, carry out, consecrate as priest (252)

מָלֵא (adj) full, filled (61)

מְלֹא fullness, abundance (38)

מִלֻּאִים consecration, ordination (of a priest), setting (of stones) (15)

מַלְאָךְ messenger, angel (213)

מְלָאכָה work, occupation, service (167)

מִלָּה word, speech (38)

מְלוּכָה kingship, royalty (24)

מֶ֫לַח salt (23)

מִלְחָמָה war, battle, struggle (319)

מָלַט (Ni) to escape, flee to safety, slip away; (Pi) let someone escape, save someone, leave undisturbed (94)

מָלַךְ (Q) to be(come) king or queen, reign, rule; (Hi) make someone king or queen, install someone as king or queen (350)

מֶ֫לֶךְ king, ruler (2,530)

מַלְכָּה queen (35)

מַלְכוּת kingdom, dominion, royal power (91)

מִמְכָּר something sold, merchandise, sale (10)

מַמְלָכָה kingdom, dominion, reign (117)

מֶמְשָׁלָה rule, dominion, authority (17)

מִן (prep) from, out of; also spelled · מִ (Nun assimilates as Daghesh Forte) when prefixed to another word (7,592)

מָן manna (13)

מָנָה (Q) to count, number, reckon, assign, appoint (28)

מָנָה part, portion, share (12)

מְנוּחָה rest, resting place (21)

מְנוֹרָה lampstand (42)

מִנְחָה gift, offering, tribute (211)

מָנַע (Q) to withhold, hold back, retain, refuse, restrain (29)

מַס forced labor (23)

מִסְגֶּ֫רֶת rim, border, fortress, prison (18)

מָסָךְ cover, curtain (25)

מַסֵּכָה molten (metal) image, idol (26)

מְסִלָּה highway, main road (27)

מָסַס (Ni) to melt (away), dissolve, become weak (21)

מַסַּע breaking camp, setting out, journey (12)

מִסְפֵּד wailing, mourning, funeral ceremony (16)

מִסְפָּר number (134)

מִסְתָּר secret place, hiding place (10)

מַעְגָּל path, wagon track (13)

מֵעֶה (ms) stomach, womb, entrails (32)

מָעוֹז refuge, stronghold; (mp) מָעֻזִּים (37)

מָעוֹן dwelling place, habitation, refuge (17)

מָעַט (Q) to be(come) few or too small; (Hi) make small or few, diminish, reduce, collect or gather little (22)

מְעַט (adj) little, few (101)

מְעִיל robe, cloak (28)

מַעְיָן spring, fountain (23)

מָעַל (Q) to be unfaithful, act unfaithfully or treacherously (36)

מַ֫עַל above, upward, on top of (140)

מַ֫עַל unfaithfulness, infidelity (29)

מַעֲלָה ascent, step, stairs (49)

מַעֲלֶה ascent, stairs, rise (22)

מַעֲלָל deed, act (42)

מַעֲרָב west, sunset (14)

מְעָרָה cave (41)

מַעֲרָכָה row, battle line (19)

מַעֲרֶ֫כֶת row (of bread), consecrated bread (10)

מַעֲשֶׂה (ms) work, deed, act (235)

מַעֲשֵׂר tithe, tenth (32)

מָצָא (Q) to find (out), reach, obtain, achieve; (Ni) be found (457)

מַצָּב military garrison, station (10)

מַצֵּבָה sacred stone, pillar (33)

מְצָד (fs) stronghold, fortress (12)

מַצָּה unleavened bread (53)

מְצוּדָה (mountain) stronghold, fortress (18)

מִצְוָה commandment; (fp) מִצְוֹת (184); מִצְוֹת יְהוָה "the commandments of Yahweh"

מָצוֹר distress, siege, affliction (20)

מֵ֫צַח forehead, brow (13)

מְצִלְתַּ֫יִם (cd) cymbals (13)

מִצְנֶ֫פֶת turban, headband, diadem (12)

מִקְדָּשׁ sanctuary (75)

מָקוֹם place, location; (mp) מְקֹמוֹת (401)

מָקוֹר spring, fountain (18)

מַקֵּל (cs) rod, staff, branch; (cp) מַקְלוֹת (18)

מִקְלָט refuge, asylum (20)

מִקְנֶה cattle, livestock, property (76)

מִקְנָה purchase, acquisition (15)

מִקְצוֹעַ corner, angle (12)

מָקַק (Ni) to rot (away), fester (wounds), dwindle or waste away, decay, melt, dissolve (10)

מִקְרָא summons, assembly (23)

מִקְרֶה (ms) accident, chance, fate (10)

מֹר myrrh, myrrh oil (12)

מַר (adj) bitter; (n) bitterness (38)

מַרְאָה appearance, vision (12)

מַרְאֶה vision, sight, appearance (103)

מְרַאֲשׁוֹת (fp) at the head of, headrest (13)

מָרַד (Q) to rebel, revolt (25)

מָרָה (Q) to be rebellious, obstinate or contentious; (Hi) behave rebelliously or obstinately (44)

מָרוֹם height, elevation, pride (54)

מֶרְחָק distance, distant place (18)

מָרַט (Q) to make smooth, bare, bald, polish, scour, pull out (hair), sharpen (sword); (Pu) be polished, smooth, bare (14)

מְרִי rebellion (23)

מֶרְכָּבָה chariot (44)

מִרְמָה deceit, deception (39)

מִרְעֶה (ms) pasture, place of grazing (13)

מַרְעִית pasture, place of grazing (10)

מַרְפֵּא healing, cure, remedy (13)

מָרַר (Q) to be bitter (of taste, experience or attitude), desperate; (Hi) embitter, cause bitterness or grief (16)

מַשָּׂא load, burden (44)

מַשָּׂא	oracle, pronouncement (20)
מַשְׂאֵת	gift, tribute (15)
מִשְׂגָּב	fortress, refuge, high point (17)
מָשׂוֹשׂ	joy, delight (16)
מַשְׂכִּיל	uncertain technical term, perhaps indicating a song of wisdom or insight (14)
מְשׁוּבָה	backsliding, falling away, apostasy (13)
מָשַׁח	(Q) to smear (with a liquid, oil or dye), anoint (with oil) (70)
מִשְׁחָה	anointing (21)
מַשְׁחִית	destroyer, destruction (10)
מָשִׁיחַ	(adj) anointed; (n) anointed one, Messiah (38)
מָשַׁךְ	(Q) to draw (out), pull, drag, prolong, stretch (36)
מִשְׁכָּב	bed, couch (46)
מִשְׁכָּן	dwelling place, tabernacle; (mp) מִשְׁכָּנוֹת (139)
מָשַׁל	(Q) to rule, reign, govern, have dominion (81)
מָשַׁל	(Q) to use a proverb, to speak in parables or poetry; (Ni) be(come) like, similar or the same as (17)
מָשָׁל	proverb, wisdom saying (40)
מִשְׁמָר	prison, guard(ing), custody, watch (22)
מִשְׁמֶ֫רֶת	watch, guard, responsibility (78)
מִשְׁנֶה	(ms) double, second (35)
מִשְׁעֶ֫נֶת	staff, stick, support (11)
מִשְׁפָּחָה	family, clan (304)
מִשְׁפָּט	judgment, decision, ordinance, law, custom (425)
מַשְׁקֶה	(ms) cupbearer, drink (19)
מִשְׁקָל	weight (49)

מָשַׁשׁ (Q) to feel, touch; (Pi) feel (over, through), grope, search, rummage through (10)

מִשְׁתֶּה (ms) feast, banquet (46)

מָתוֹק (adj) sweet, pleasant (12)

מָתַי when? (43)

מְתִים (mp) men; מְתֵי מִסְפָּר few in number (22)

מַתָּנָה gift, present (17)

מָתְנַיִם (md) hips, waist, loins (47)

נ

נָא (emphatic particle) please, now, surely (405)

נָאוֶה (adj) lovely, beautiful, desirable, suitable (10)

נְאֻם utterance, announcement, revelation (376); נְאֻם־יְהוָה "says (declares) Yahweh"

נָאַף (Q) to commit adultery; (metaphorically) commit idolatry; (Pi) commit adultery (31)

נָאַץ (Q) to spurn, despise; (Pi) treat disrespectfully or with irreverence (24)

נָבָא (Ni) to prophesy, be in a state of prophetic ecstasy; (Hith) speak or behave as a prophet (115)

נָבַט (Hi) to look (at or out), gaze, behold (70)

נָבִיא prophet (317)

נָבֵל (Q) to fade, wither, decay, crumble away, wear out (20)

נֵבֶל stringed instrument, harp (28)

נֵבֶל jar, bottle (10)

נָבָל (adj) foolish, good-for-nothing; (n) fool (18)

נְבָלָה outrage, disgrace, stupidity (13)

נְבֵלָה carcass, corpse (48)

נָבַע (Hi) to make (something) gush or bubble (forth), pour out or ferment (11)

נֶגֶב south, southward, Negev (29)

נָגַד (Hi) to tell, announce, report, declare, inform; (Hoph) be told, announced, reported (371)

נֶגֶד (prep) opposite, in front of (151)

נֹגַהּ brightness, radiance (19)

נָגַח (Q) to gore (ox as subject); (Pi) push, butt, thrust, knock down (11)

נָגִיד leader, ruler (44)

נְגִינָה music of a stringed instrument, song of mockery (14)

נָגַן (Pi) to play a stringed instrument (15)

נָגַע (Q) to touch, strike, reach; (Hi) touch, reach, throw, arrive (150)

נֶגַע plague, affliction (78)

נָגַף (Q) to smite, strike, injure; (Ni) be smitten, struck (with) (49)

נָגַר (Ni) to flow, gush forth, be poured (out), spilled, stretched out (hands); (Hi) pour (out, down) (10)

נָגַשׂ (Q) to oppress, force to work, be a slave driver or taskmaster, exact (contributions), collect (offerings) (23)

נָגַשׁ (Q) to draw near, approach; (Ni) draw near; (Hi) bring (near), offer (a sacrifice) (125)

נָדַב (Q) to incite, instigate; (Hith) volunteer, make a voluntary decision, offer voluntarily, give a freewill offering (17)

נְדָבָה freewill offering, voluntary gift (26)

נָדַד (Q) to flee, wander (about), depart, move, flutter (wings) (28)

נִדָּה menstrual flow, impurity, defilement (29)

נָדַח (Ni) to be scattered, banished, driven away, thrust out; (Hi) scatter, drive away, disperse, thrust out (51)

נָדִיב (adj) noble, willing, generous (26)

נָדַר (Q) to make (perform) a vow, keep (make) a promise (31)

נֶ֫דֶר vow; also spelled נֵ֫דֶר (60)

נָהַג (Q) to drive (flocks or herds), lead, guide; (Pi) lead or drive away (30)

נָהַל (Pi) to lead, guide, escort, provide (with food) (10)

נָהָר river, stream; (mp) נְהָרוֹת and נְהָרִים (119)

נוּד (Q) to move to and fro, sway, wander, be(come) aimless, express grief or sympathy (by shaking the head) (25)

נָוֶה (ms) pasture, dwelling (32)

נָוָה pasture, dwelling; (fp cstr) נְאוֹת (15)

נוּחַ (Q) to rest, settle down, repose; (Hi) cause to rest, secure rest, set, leave (behind or untouched) (140)

נוּס (Q) to flee, escape (160)

נוּעַ (Q) to tremble, shake, totter, wave (of trees); (Hi) make unstable or unsteady, shake (up), disturb (42)

נוּף (Hi) to move back and forth, wave, brandish, wield (34)

נָזָה (Q) to spatter (blood); (Hi) sprinkle (24)

נָזִיר one who is devoted or consecrated, a Nazirite (16)

נָזַל (Q) to trickle, drip down, flow (16)

נֶ֫זֶם earring, nose-ring (17)

נָזַר (Ni) to devote, dedicate or consecrate oneself to (a deity), treat with awe, deal respectfully with; (Hi) restrain from, abstain from, live as a Nazirite (10)

נֵ֫זֶר consecration, dedication, crown (25)

נָחָה (Q) to lead; (Hi) lead, guide, conduct (39)

נְחוּשָׁה copper, bronze (10)

נָחַל (Q) to take (as a) possession, obtain (receive) property, give as an inheritance; (Hi) give as an inheritance (59)

נַ֫חַל stream, brook, wadi (137)

נַחֲלָה inheritance, property, possession (222)

נָחַם (Ni) to be sorry, regret, have compassion (on or for); (Pi) comfort, console (108)

נָחַשׁ (Pi) to practice divination, seek and give omens, observe signs, foretell, predict (11)

נָחָשׁ serpent, snake (31)

נְחֹ֫שֶׁת copper, bronze (139)

נָטָה (Q) to spread out, stretch out, extend, pitch (a tent), turn, bend; (Hi) turn, incline, stretch out, spread out (216)

נָטַע (Q) to plant (59)

נָטַף (Q) to drop, drip, secrete; (Hi) cause to drip, cause to flow (metaphorically, of prophetic speech) (18)

נָטַשׁ (Q) to leave, forsake, abandon, give up (something); (Ni) be forsaken (40)

נִיחֹחַ soothing or pleasing scent; also spelled נִיחוֹחַ (43)

נָכָה (Hi) to strike, smite, beat, strike dead, destroy; (Hoph) be struck down dead, beaten (501)

נֹכַח (prep) in front of, opposite (25)

נָכַר (Hi) to recognize, know, investigate, be acquainted with, acknowledge (50)

נֵכָר foreigner, stranger (36)

נָכְרִי (adj) foreign, strange; (fs) נָכְרִיָּה (46)

נֵס flag, banner (21)

נָסָה (Pi) to test, put someone to the test, tempt (36)

נָסַךְ (Q) to pour out, pour (cast) a metal image or statue; (Hi) pour out libations, offer a drink offering (25)

נֶ֫סֶךְ drink offering; also spelled נֵ֫סֶךְ (60)

נָסַע (Q) to pull (out or up), set out, start out, depart, journey (146)

נְעוּרִים youth (46)

נָעִים (adj) pleasant, lovely, delightful (13)

נַ֫עַל (fs) sandal, shoe (22)

נָעַר (Q, Pi) to shake (out or off); (Ni) be shaken (out or off) (11)

נַ֫עַר boy, youth, servant (240)

נַעֲרָה young girl, newly married woman, maidservant (76)

נָפַח (Q) to breathe, blow, blow fire upon, set aflame, gasp, pant (12)

נָפַל (Q) to fall, fall upon; (Hi) cause to fall, bring to ruin (435)

נָפַץ (Q) to shatter, smash to pieces; (Pi) smash (19)

נֶ֫פֶשׁ (fs) soul, life, person, neck, throat (757)

נָצַב (Ni) to stand (firm), take one's stand, station oneself, be positioned; (Hi) station, set (up), place, establish (74)

נָצַח (Pi) to supervise, oversee or inspect works and activities related to the temple; מְנַצֵּחַ (ptc) used as title (superscription) in 55 psalms (65)

נֶ֫צַח forever, everlasting (43)

נְצִיב pillar, post, military garrison (12)

נָצַל (Ni) to be rescued, delivered, saved; (Hi) tear from, take away, deliver from (213)

נָצַר (Q) to keep watch, watch over, guard, protect, preserve (63)

נָקַב (Q) to pierce, bore (through), stipulate, specify, designate, curse, slander (19)

נְקֵבָה female, woman (22)

נָקָה (Ni) to be free (of), without guilt, innocent, exempt from (punishment); (Pi) leave unpunished, regard as innocent (44)

נָקִי (adj) blameless, innocent (43)

נָקַם (Q) to avenge, take vengeance (on), take revenge; (Ni) avenge oneself, take revenge (35)

נָקָם vengeance, revenge (17)

נְקָמָה vengeance, revenge (27)

נָקַף (Hi) to surround, go around, encircle, encompass, enclose (17)

נֵר lamp, light; (mp) נֵרוֹת (44)

נָשָׂא (Q) to lift, carry, raise, bear (load or burden), take (away); (Ni) be carried, lifted up, exalted; (Pi) lift up, exalt; (Hith) lift oneself up, exalt oneself (659)

נָשַׂג (Hi) to reach, overtake (50)

נָשִׂיא chief, leader, prince (130)

נָשָׁא (Hi) to deceive, cheat, trick (14)

נָשָׁה (Q) to forget (18)

נֶ֫שֶׁךְ interest, usury (12)

נָשַׁךְ (Q, Pi) to bite (11)

נְשָׁמָה breath (24)

נֶ֫שֶׁף twilight, dusk (12)

נָשַׁק (Q) to kiss (32)

נֶ֫שֶׁר eagle, vulture (26)

נֵ֫תַח piece of meat (13)

נְתִיבָה path, way (21)

נָתִין temple servant (17)

נָתַךְ (Q) to gush forth, pour out; (Ni) gush forth, be poured (out or forth) (21)

נָתַן (Q) to give, put, place, set; (Ni) be given (2,014)

נָתַץ (Q) to tear down, pull down, break down, demolish (42)

נָתַק (Q) to pull off, tear away; (Ni) be drawn out or away, torn apart; (Pi) tear apart, tear to pieces (27)

נֶ֫תֶק skin disease, scab (14)

נָתַשׁ (Q) to uproot, pull out, extract, pull up, remove, drive out (nations) (21)

ס

סָבַב (Q) to turn (about), go around, surround; (Ni) turn; (Hi) cause to go around, lead around; (Polel) encompass with protection (163)

סָבִיב around, about; (substantive) surroundings (338)

סָגָן official, ruler (17)

סָגַר (Q) to shut (in), close; (Hi) deliver (up), hand over, surrender, give up (91)

סוּג (Q) to backslide, be disloyal; (Ni) turn back, withdraw, become disloyal (24)

סוֹד confidential conversation, circle of confidants (21)

סוּךְ (Q) to grease (oneself) with oil, anoint (10)

סוּס horse (138)

סוּף reed, (coll) reeds; יַם־סוּף "Sea of Reeds" (or "Red Sea") (28)

סוּפָה wind (of a storm), tempest, gale (15)

סוּר (Q) to turn (aside), turn off, leave (off), desist; (Hi) remove, take away, get rid of (298)

סוּת (Hi) to incite (against), stir up, provoke, instigate, seduce, mislead, lead astray (18)

סָחַר (Q) to pass through (of shepherds), travel about (conducting business); (Q ptc) trader, merchant (21)

סִיר (cs) basin, pot, tub (29)

סֻכָּה booth, tabernacle (31)

סָכַךְ (Q) to overshadow, cover (protectively), protect (16)

סָכַן (Q) to be of use or service; (Hi) be accustomed to, familiar (acquainted) with, in the habit of (13)

סַל basket (15)

סֶלָה technical poetic notation of undetermined meaning (74)

סָלַח (Q) to pardon, forgive; (Ni) be forgiven (47)

סָלַל (Q) to pile up, heap up, lift up, exalt, praise (12)

סֹלְלָה mound, siege ramp (11)

סֶלַע rock, stone, cliff (59)

סֹלֶת flour (53)

סַם perfume, spices (16)

סָמַךְ (Q) to support, uphold, sustain, help, lean or lay (hand upon); (Ni) lean (on or against), support oneself (48)

סָעַד (Q) to support, sustain, strengthen (with food), uphold (12)

סְעָרָה windstorm, tempest, gale (18)

סַף threshold, doorframe (25)

סָפַד (Q) to lament, wail, bewail, mourn for someone (30)

סָפָה (Q) to take, sweep, snatch or carry away; (Ni) be carried, swept or snatched away (19)

סַפִּיר sapphire, lapis lazuli (11)

סָפַר (Q) to count; (Pi) count, recount, make known, proclaim, report, tell (107)

סֵ֫פֶר book, scroll, document (191); סֵפֶר הַתּוֹרָה "the book of the law"

סֹפֵר scribe, secretary (54)

סָקַל (Q) to stone, put to death by stoning; (Ni) be stoned (to death) (22)

סָרִיס official, eunuch (45)

סֶ֫רֶן ruler, lord (21)

סָרַר (Q) to be stubborn or rebellious (17)

סָתַם (Q) to plug or stop up, shut up, close, hide, keep secret, disguise (13)

סָתַר (Ni) to be hidden, hide oneself; (Hi) hide (82)

סֵ֫תֶר hiding place, secret place, shelter (35)

ע

עָב cloud, clouds (31)

עָבַד (Q) to work, serve, toil (289)

עֶ֫בֶד slave, servant (803)

עֲבֹדָה work, labor, service, worship (145)

עָבַר (Q) to pass over, pass through, pass by, cross; (Hi) cause to pass over, bring over, cause or allow to pass (through), cause to pass through fire, sacrifice (553)

עֵבֶר beyond, other side, edge, bank (92)

עֶבְרָה wrath, anger, fury (34)

עֲבֹת (cs) cord, rope; (cp) עֲבֹתֹת and עֲבֹתִים (19)

עֵגֶל calf, young bull (35)

עֲגָלָה cart, wagon (25)

עֶגְלָה heifer, young cow (12)

עֵד witness (69)

עַד (prep) until, as far as (1,263)

עַד forever, eternal; spelled וָעֶד with conjunction וְ (47)

עֵדָה congregation, assembly (171)

עֵדוּת witness, testimony; (fp) עֵדוֹת (61)

עֲדִי ornament, jewelry; (with 3ms suff) עֶדְיוֹ (14)

עֵדֶר flock, herd (38)

עוֹד again, still, as long as (491)

עוּד (Hi) to warn, admonish, witness, be a witness, testify (40)

עָוָה (Q) to do wrong; (Ni) be disturbed or irritated; (Hi) twist, pervert, do wrong (17)

עָוֶל iniquity, injustice, wrong (21)

עַוְלָה iniquity, injustice, wickedness (34)

עוֹלֵל child (11)

עוֹלָם forever, everlasting, ancient; also spelled עֹלָם (439)

עָוֹן transgression, iniquity, guilt, punishment (of sin); (mp) עֲוֹנוֹת (233)

עוֹף (coll) flying creatures, birds, insects (71)

עוּף (Q) to fly (27)

עוֹר skin, hide, leather (99)

עִוֵּר (adj) blind; (mp) עִוְרִים (26)

עוּר (Q) to be awake, stir up; (Hi) arouse, rouse, wake up, stir up; (Polel) arouse, disturb, awaken (80)

עָוַת (Q) to bend, make crooked, pervert (justice), falsify (balances), suppress (12)

עַז (adj) strong, mighty (23)

עֵז (fs) goat, goat's hair; (fp) עִזִּים (74)

עֹז strength, power, might; (with 3ms suff) עֻזּוֹ (76)

עֹז refuge, protection (17)

עָזַב (Q) to leave, leave behind, forsake, abandon, set free (214)

עָזַז (Q) to be strong, prevail (against), defy (11)

עָזַר (Q) to help, assist, come to the aid of (82)

עֵ֫זֶר help, assistance (17)

עֶזְרָה help, assistance, support (26)

עָטָה (Q) to wrap, cover or envelop (oneself) with (13)

עָטַף (Q) to be(come) weak, feeble or faint; (Hith) feel weak or faint (11)

עֲטָרָה crown, wreath; (fs cstr) עֲטֶ֫רֶת (23)

עַ֫יִן (cs) eye, spring (900)

עָיֵף (adj) tired, exhausted, weary (17)

עִיר (fs) city, town; (fp) עָרִים (1,088)

עֵירֹם (adj) naked; (n) nakedness (10)

עָכַר (Q) to disturb, trouble, confuse, bring disaster (ruin); be stirred up, ruined, cut off (14)

עֹל yoke; (with 3ms suff) עֻלּוֹ (40)

עַל (prep) on, upon, on account of, according to (5,777)

עָלָה (Q) to go up, ascend; (Ni) be taken up; (Hi) bring or lead up or out, offer up (sacrifice) (894)

עֹלָה whole burnt offering (sacrifice that is completely burned) (286)

עָלֶה (ms) leaf, foliage (19)

עָלַז (Q) to exult, triumph (17)

עֲלִיָּה upper room, roof chamber (20)

עֶלְיוֹן (adj) upper; (divine title) Most High (53)

עֲלִילָה deed, action (24)

עָלַל (Poel) to deal or act severely with, treat violently, glean (19)

עָלַם (Ni) to be concealed, hidden; (Hi) conceal, hide, cover up; (Hith) hide oneself (28)

עַם people; (mp) עַמִּים (1,869)

עִם (prep) with, together with; (with 3ms suff) עִמּוֹ (1,048)

עָמַד (Q) to stand (up), take one's stand, stand still; (Hi) station, set up, appoint, designate (524)

עִמָּד (prep) with (45)

עַמּוּד pillar, column, tent pole (112)

עָמִית (ms) neighbor, friend, community (12)

עָמַל (Q) to labor, toil, exert oneself (12)

עָמָל trouble, labor, toil (54)

עָמֹק (adj) deep, unfathomable, mysterious; (fs) עֲמֻקָּה (17)

עֵ֫מֶק valley, plain (70)

עֵנָב grape (19)

עָנַג (Hith) to pamper oneself, take delight (pleasure) in, refresh oneself (10)

עָנָה (Q) to answer, respond, reply, testify; (Ni) be answered (316)

עָנָה (Q) to be afflicted, humbled; (Pi) afflict, oppress, humiliate, violate (79)

עָנָה (Q) to sing (16)

עָנָו (adj) afflicted, oppressed, humble, meek (25)

עָנִי (adj) poor, humble, afflicted (80)

עֳנִי poverty, affliction, misery (36)

עָנָן (coll) clouds (87)

עָנַן (Poel) to practice soothsaying, conjure up (spirits), interpret signs (11)

עַפְעַפַּ֫יִם (md) eyelids, eyes (10)

עָפָר dust, dry earth (110)

עֵץ tree, wood (330)

עָצָב idol, image, false god; (always mp) עֲצַבִּים (17)

עָצַב (Q) to hurt, pain, rebuke, grieve; (Ni) be pained for, in grieving for, worried, distressed (15)

עֵצָה counsel, plan, advice (87)

עָצוּם (adj) mighty, numerous (31)

עָצֵל (adj) low, lazy; (n) sluggard (14)

עָצַם (Q) to be vast, mighty, powerful or numerous (17)

עֶ֫צֶם (fs) bone, skeleton (126)

עָצַר (Q) to hold back, restrain, hinder, imprison; (Ni) be restrained, shut up, detained (46)

עֲצָרָה assembly, celebration; also spelled עֲצֶ֫רֶת (11)

עָקֵב heel, footprint, rear guard (of an army) (14)

עֵ֫קֶב because, on account of; (n) result, wages (15)

עָקָר (adj) barren, childless (12)

עִקֵּשׁ (adj) perverted, crooked, false (10)

עָרַב (Q) to stand as surety for, pledge oneself (as surety for debts), be responsible for someone, conduct trade, barter (17)

עֹרֵב raven (10)

עֶ֫רֶב evening, sunset (134)

עֲרָבָה desert plain, Arabah (60)

עָרָה (Pi) to uncover, reveal, expose, lay bare, empty; (Hi) uncover, make naked, expose (15)

עֶרְוָה nakedness (54)

עָרוּם (adj) crafty, cunning, clever, prudent (11)

עָרוֹם (adj) naked (16)

עָרִיץ (adj) ruthless, fierce, violent (20)

עָרַךְ (Q) to set in order, lay out, set in rows, arrange, stack (wood), draw up a battle formation (75)

עֵ֫רֶךְ value, assessment (33)

עָרֵל (adj) uncircumcised (35)

עָרְלָה foreskin (16)

עֲרֵמָה heap, mound (of grain) (11)

עֹ֫רֶף (back of) neck (33)

עֲרָפֶל thick darkness, gloom (15)

עָרַץ (Q) to tremble, be terrified, in dread, startled, alarmed; (Hi) terrify, strike (inspire) with awe (15)

עֶ֫רֶשׂ (fs) couch, bed (10)

עֵשֶׂב green plant, grass (33)

עָשָׂה (Q) to do, make; (Ni) be done, made (2,632)

עָשׂוֹר ten, tenth (day) (16)

עֲשִׂירִי (adj) tenth; (fs) עֲשִׂירִית (29)

עָשַׂר (Q) to exact a tithe, take a tenth part of; (Pi) give, pay or receive a tenth, tithe (10)

עָשָׂר ten; (fs) עֶשְׂרֵה; used in constructions to express numerals eleven to nineteen (337)

עֶשֶׂר ten; (fs) עֲשָׂרָה; (mp) עֶשְׂרִים twenty, twentieth (492)

עִשָּׂרוֹן tenth part; (mp) עֶשְׂרֹנִים (33)

עָשִׁיר (adj) rich, wealthy (23)

עָשָׁן smoke (25)

עֹשֶׁק oppression, extortion (15)

עָשַׁק (Q) to oppress, exploit, wrong (someone) (37)

עָשַׁר (Q) to be(come) rich; (Hi) make rich, gain riches (17)

עֹשֶׁר wealth, riches (37)

עַשְׁתֵּי eleven, eleventh (19); always in the construction עַשְׁתֵּי־עָשָׂר or עַשְׁתֵּי־עֶשְׂרֵה

עֵת (cs) time, point of time; (cp) עִתִּים and עִתּוֹת (296)

עַתָּה now, after all, at last, then (435)

עַתּוּד male goat, leader (29)

עָתַר (Q) to pray, plead, entreat; (Ni) be entreated; (Hi) pray, plead (20)

פ

פֵּאָה corner, side, cdge (86)

פָּאַר (Pi) to glorify, exalt, beautify; (Hith) show or manifest one’s glory, glorify oneself, be glorified, boast (13)

פָּגַע (Q) to meet, encounter, fall upon, attack, assail, reach (46)

פֶּ֫גֶר corpse, carcass (22)

פָּגַשׁ (Q) to meet, encounter, confront (14)

פָּדָה (Q) to ransom, redeem, buy out (60)

פֹּה here, at this place; also spelled פּוֹ (82)

פֶּה (ms) mouth, opening; (ms cstr) פִּי (498)

פּוּחַ (Hi) to testify (10)

פּוּץ (Q) to be spread, dispersed, scattered, overflow; (Ni) be scattered, dispersed; (Hi) scatter, disperse (65)

פָּזַר (Pi) to scatter, disperse (10)

פַּח snare, trap, net (25)

פָּחַד (Q) to tremble, shiver, be startled, in dread, in awe (25)

פַּ֫חַד trembling, terror, dread (49)

פֶּחָה governor (28)

פַּ֫חַת pit, ravine (10)

פֶּ֫טֶר firstborn (11)

פִּילֶ֫גֶשׁ (fs) concubine; (fp) פִּילַגְשִׁים (37)

פָּלָא (Ni) to be extraordinary, wonderful; (Hi) do something wonderful (71)

פֶּ֫לֶא wonder, miracle, something extraordinary (13)

פֶּ֫לֶג water channel, canal (10)

פָּלַט (Pi) to bring out, bring forth, bring to safety, save (27)

פָּלִיט fugitive, survivor (19)

פְּלֵיטָה survivor, escape, deliverance (28)

פָּלַל (Hith) to pray, make intercession (84)

פֶּן־ lest, otherwise (133)

פָּנָה (Q) to turn (toward, from, to the side, away) (134)

פִּנָּה corner, cornerstone (30)

פָּנִים (cp) face, front; לִפְנֵי (prep לְ prefixed to cstr) before, in front of (2,126)

פְּנִימָה inside, within (14)

פְּנִימִי (adj) inner; (fs) פְּנִימִית (32)

פֶּ֫סַח Passover (49)

פִּסֵּחַ (adj) lame, crippled (14)

פָּסִיל idol, cultic statue (23)

פֶּ֫סֶל idol, carved image (31)

פָּעַל (Q) to do, make, perform (58)

פֹּ֫עַל work, deed (36)

פְּעֻלָּה work, deed, reward, payment (14)

פַּ֫עַם (fs) foot, pace, time; (fp) פְּעָמִים (118)

פָּצָה (Q) to open (the mouth), speak (15)

פָּקַד (Q) to attend (to), pay attention to, take care of, miss (someone), number, appoint; (Ni) be missed, visited, appointed; (Hi) appoint, entrust (304)

פְּקֻדָּה appointment, service, watch, punishment (32)

פִּקּוּדִים precepts, directions, instructions (24)

פָּקַח (Q) to open (the) eyes (21)

פָּקִיד leader, overseer, officer (13)

פַּר bull, ox, steer (133)

פֶּ֫רֶא wild donkey (10)

פָּרַד (Ni) to divide, separate (intransitive), be scattered, separated (26)

פֶּ֫רֶד mule (14)

פָּרָה (Q) to bear fruit, be fruitful (29)

פָּרָה cow (26)

פֶּ֫רַח blossom, bud, flower (17)

פָּרַח (Q) to bud, sprout, bloom, shoot, break out, break open (34)

פְּרִי fruit, offspring (119)

פָּרֹ֫כֶת curtain (25)

פָּרַס (Q) to break; (Hi) have a divided hoof (14)

פַּרְסָה hoof (21)

פָּרַע (Q) to let go, loose or free, let the hair of the head hang loose, allow to run wild, leave unattended (16)

פָּרַץ (Q) to break through (out or into), make a breach, burst open, spread out (46)

פֶּ֫רֶץ breach, gap (19)

פָּרַק (Q) to tear away, pull away, rescue; (Pi) pull or tear off; (Hith) pull or tear off from oneself, be pulled or torn off (10)

פָּרַר (Hi) to break (out), destroy, put an end to, make ineffectual (47)

פָּרַשׂ (Q) to spread out (as with hands in prayer), stretch (out or over) (67)

פָּרָשׁ horseman, horse (57)

פָּשָׂה (Q) to spread (the symptoms of disease) (22)

פָּשַׁט (Q) to take off (clothes), strip off, rush out, make a raid; (Hi) take off (clothes or armor), strip off (skin), flay (43)

פָּשַׁע (Q) to revolt, rebel (against), transgress, break with, break away from, behave as a criminal (41)

פֶּ֫שַׁע transgression, rebellion (93)

פֵּ֫שֶׁת linen, flax; (fp) פִּשְׁתִּים (16)

פַּת piece, scrap, morsel; (fp) פִּתִּים (14)

פִּתְאֹם suddenly, unexpectedly (25)

פָּתָה (Q) to be simple, inexperienced or gullible; (Pi) fool, deceive, persuade, seduce (27)

פִּתּוּחַ engraving, inscription (11)

פֶּ֫תַח opening, entrance, doorway (164)

פָּתַח (Q) to open (up); (Ni) be opened, loosened, set free; (Pi) let loose, loosen (136)

פֶּ֫תִי naïve person, simpleton; (mp) פְּתָאיִם (17)

פָּתִיל cord, thread (11)

צ

צֹאן (cs) flock(s), flock of sheep and goats (274)

צֶאֱצָאִים offspring, descendants (11)

צָבָא (cs) host, army, war, service; (cp) צְבָאוֹת (487); יְהוָה צְבָאוֹת "Lord of Hosts"

צָבָא (Q) to wage war, go to war, fight against (14)

צְבִי ornament, something beautiful, splendor (18)

צְבִי gazelle (12)

צַד side; (mp) צִדִּים (33)

צַדִּיק (adj) righteous, just, innocent (206)

צָדַק (Q) to be in the right, have a just cause, be just (justified), be righteous; (Hi) justify, declare righteous, just or innocent (41)

צֶ֫דֶק righteousness, equity (123)

צְדָקָה righteousness, righteous act, justice (159)

צָהֳרַ֫יִם noon, midday (23)

צַוָּאר neck (41)

צוּד (Q) to hunt (17)

צָוָה (Pi) to command, give an order, charge; (Pu) be ordered, be told, receive a command (496)

צוּם (Q) to fast, abstain from food and drink (21)

צוֹם fast, (period of) fasting (26)

צוּק (Hi) to oppress, press hard, harass, constrain (12)

צוּר rock, boulder (73)

צוּר (Q) to tie up, bind, shut in, shut up, enclose, encircle, besiege (31)

צָחַק (Q) to laugh; (Pi) joke (with), play (with), amuse oneself, fondle (13)

צַ֫יִד game, hunting, hunter (14)

צֵידָה food, provisions (10)

צִיָּה desert, dry land (16)

צִיץ flower, blossom; (mp) צִצִּים (14)

צֵל shadow, shade, protection (53)

צָלַח (Q) to succeed, prosper, be successful; (Hi) be successful, succeed, cause to succeed or prosper (65)

צֶ֫לֶם image, idol (15)

צַלְמָ֫וֶת (ms) shadow of death, deep darkness, gloom (18)

צֵלָע (fs) rib, side (40)

צָמָא thirst (17)

צָמֵא (Q) to thirst, be thirsty (10)

צֶ֫מֶד pair, team (15)

צָמַח (Q) to sprout, spring up, grow; (Hi) make grow or sprout (33)

צֶ֫מַח growth, sprout, branch (12)

צֶ֫מֶר wool (16)

צָמַת (Hi) to silence, exterminate, annihilate (15)

צִנָּה large shield (20)

צַעַד step, pace (14)

צָעִיר (adj) little, small, young (23)

צָעַק (Q) to shout, cry (out), call for help; (Ni) be called together, summoned (55)

צְעָקָה outcry, wailing (21)

צָפָה (Pi) to overlay, plate (with gold) (47)

צָפָה (Q) to keep watch, watch attentively, spy (37)

צָפוֹן (fs) north, northern (153)

צִפּוֹר (cs) bird; (cp) צִפֳּרִים (40)

צָפַן (Q) to hide, store (up), treasure (up), keep (34)

צְפַרְדֵּעַ (fs) frog; (fp) צְפַרְדְּעִים (13)

צַר adversary, enemy (72)

צַר (adj) narrow; (n) anxiety, distress (27)

צָרָה distress, anxiety, trouble (70)

צָרַע (Q) to be afflicted with a skin disease (usually leprosy); (Pu) be struck with a skin disease (20)

צָרַעַת leprosy, skin disease (35)

צָרַף (Q) to smelt (metal), refine (by smelting), test (34)

צָרַר (Q) to wrap (up), tie up, bind (transitive); be cramped, restricted, depressed (intransitive); (Hi) oppress, harass, afflict (47)

צָרַר (Q) to be hostile (toward), treat with hostility, attack (26)

ק

קָבַב (Q) to curse (14)

קְבוּרָה grave, burial (14)

קָבַל (Pi) to take, receive, accept (14)

קָבַץ (Q) to collect, gather, assemble; (Ni) be gathered, assembled; (Pi) gather together, assemble (127)

קָבַר (Q) to bury; (Ni) be buried (133)

קֶ֫בֶר grave, burial site; (mp) קְבָרִים and קְבָרוֹת (67)

קָדַד (Q) to bow down, kneel down (15)

קָדוֹשׁ (adj) holy, set apart (117)

קָדִים east, eastern, east wind (69)

קָדַם (Pi) to be in front, confront, meet, go before, walk at the head, do something early or for the first time (26)

קֶ֫דֶם east, ancient times (61)

קֵ֫דְמָה eastward, toward the east (26); קֶ֫דֶם plus directional ה

קַדְמֹנִי (adj) eastern, former, past (10)

קָדְקֹד crown of the head, skull (11)

קָדַר (Q) to be(come) dark, dirty, untidy, dressed in the clothes of mourning (17)

קָדַשׁ (Q) to be holy, set apart or consecrated; (Ni) be honored or treated as holy; (Pi) set apart, consecrate or dedicate as holy; (Hi) consecrate, dedicate or declare as holy; (Hith) show or keep oneself holy (171)

קֹ֫דֶשׁ holiness, something that is holy (470)

קָדֵשׁ cult or temple prostitute (11)

קָהַל (Ni) to assemble, meet together (intransitive); (Hi) assemble (transitive), summon (39)

קָהָל assembly, community, crowd (123)

קַו measuring line (13)

קָוָה (Pi) to wait (for), wait with eagerness, hope (47)

קוֹל voice, sound, noise; also spelled קֹל (505)

קוּם (Q) to rise, arise, get up, stand (up); (Hi) set up, put up, cause to arise, establish (627)

קוֹמָה height (46)

קוֹץ thorn, thornbush (11)

קָטֹן (adj) small, young, insignificant; (fs) קְטַנָּה (74)

קָטָן (adj) small, young, insignificant, unimportant; (mp) קְטַנִּים (27)

קָטַר (Pi) to make a sacrifice go up in smoke, offer (a sacrifice) by burning; (Hi) cause a sacrifice to go up in smoke (115)

קְטֹרֶת incense, smoke (60)

קִינָה lament, funeral song, dirge (18)

קַיִץ summer, summer fruit (20)

קִיץ (Hi) to awake, wake up (22)

קִיר wall; (mp) קִירוֹת (73)

קַל (adj) light, swift, agile (13)

קָלוֹן shame, dishonor (17)

קָלַל (Q) to be small, insignificant, of little account, swift; (Ni, Pi) declare cursed; (Hi) treat with contempt (82)

קְלָלָה curse (33)

קֶלַע curtain (16)

קָמָה standing grain (10)

קֶמַח flour (14)

קֵן nest, nestlings (13)

קָנָא (Pi) to envy, be envious of, jealous of, zealous for (34)

קִנְאָה jealousy, zeal (43)

קָנָה (Q) to get, acquire, buy (85)

קָנֶה (ms) reed (62)

קִנְיָן property, possessions (10)

קָסַם (Q) to practice divination, consult a spirit of the dead, predict (22)

קֶ֫סֶם divination, prediction (11)

קְעָרָה dish, bowl, platter (17)

קֵץ end, border, limit (67)

קָצָה end, edge, tip, boundary (35)

קָצֶה (ms) end, border, outskirts (92)

קָצִין commander, leader, ruler (12)

קָצִיר harvest (49)

קָצַף (Q) to be(come) angry or furious (34)

קֶ֫צֶף wrath, anger (28)

קָצַץ (Q) to cut (chop) off, trim; (Pi) cut (chop) off, cut in pieces (14)

קָצַר (Q) to gather in, reap, harvest (36)

קָצַר (Q) to be(come) short, shortened, impatient (14)

קָרָא (Q) to call, summon, proclaim, read aloud, give a name to; (Ni) be called, summoned, proclaimed (739)

קָרָא (Q) to meet, encounter, happen; inf cstr with prep לְ (לִקְרַאת) toward, against, opposite (136)

קָרַב (Q) to approach, draw near, come near; (Hi) bring (near), present, offer a sacrifice or offering (280)

קֶ֫רֶב inner part(s), organ(s), body; (prep) בְּקֶ֫רֶב (155x) in the middle of, among (227)

קָרֵב approaching, drawing near (12)

קָרְבָּן gift, offering (80)

קָרָה (Q) to encounter, meet, befall, happen to (22)

קָרוֹב (adj) near, close (75)

קָרְחָה baldness, bald spot (11)

קִרְיָה city, town (29)

קֶ֫רֶן (fs) horn (76)

קֶ֫רֶס (curtain) hook, clasp (10)

קָרַע (Q) to tear, rend, cut up, tear away (63)

קֶ֫רֶשׁ board, plank (51)

קַשׁ stubble, chaff (16)

קָשַׁב (Hi) to give (pay) attention, listen carefully or attentively (46)

קָשָׁה (Q) to be heavy, hard or difficult; (Hi) make hard, harden, make stubborn or obstinate (28)

קָשֶׁה (adj) difficult, hard, severe; (fs) קָשָׁה (36)

קָשַׁר (Q) to bind, be in league together, conspire (against) (44)

קֶ֫שֶׁר alliance, conspiracy, treason (16)

קֶ֫שֶׁת bow, weapon (76)

ר

רָאָה (Q) to see, perceive, understand; (Ni) appear; (Pu) be seen; (Hi) let or cause someone to see (something) (1,311)

רֹאֶה seer (11)

רֹאשׁ head, top, chief; (mp) רָאשִׁים (600)

רֹאשׁ poisonous herb, venom (12)

רִאשׁוֹן (adj) first, former; (fs) רִאשֹׁנָה ; (mp) רִאשֹׁנִים (182)

רֵאשִׁית beginning, first (51)

רֹב multitude, abundance, greatness (150)

רַב (adj) great, many; (mp) רַבִּים (419)

רַב chief, captain, ruler (30)

רָבַב (Q) to be(come) many, numerous or great (23)

רְבָבָה ten thousand, great multitude, immense number (18)

רָבָה (Q) to be(come) numerous, great, increase; (Hi) make many, make great, multiply, increase (229)

רִבּוֹא (fs) ten thousand, countless number; also spelled רִבּוֹ (11)

רְבִיעִי (adj) fourth; (fs) רְבִיעִית (55)

רָבַע (Q) to provide with four corners, make square (12)

רָבַץ (Q) to lie down, crouch (of animals), rest, stretch out (30)

רָגַז (Q) to shake, quake, tremble, be agitated, perturbed, excited, upset (41)

רָגַל (Pi) to spy (out), scout (26)

רֶ֫גֶל (fs) foot (251)

רַגְלִי (one who goes) on foot, pedestrian, foot soldier (12)

רָגַם (Q) to stone, kill by stoning (16)

רָגַע (Q) to crust over or become hard (of skin), stir up (sea); (Hi) give rest to, come to rest, make peace, linger (13)

רֶ֫גַע moment, instant (22)

רָדָה (Q) to rule (over), have dominion over, govern (with the nuance of oppression), tread (in) the winepress (22)

רָדַף (Q) to pursue, follow after, chase, persecute (144)

רָוָה (Q) to drink one's fill; (Pi, Hi) drink abundantly, water thoroughly, drench, saturate (14)

רָוַח (Q) to get relief; (Pu) be wide or spacious; (Hi) smell (14)

רוּחַ (cs) spirit, wind, breath; (cp) רוּחוֹת (378)

רוּם (Q) to be high, exalted, rise, arise; (Hi) raise, lift up, exalt, take away; (Hoph) be exalted; (Polel) exalt, bring up, extol, raise (children) (197)

רוּעַ (Hi) to shout, cry (out), shout a war cry (alarm of battle), sound a signal for war, cheer, shout in triumph (44)

רוּץ (Q) to run (104)

רוּשׁ (Q) to be poor (24)

רָחַב (Q) to open wide; (Hi) make wide or large, extend (26)

רֹחַב width, breadth, expanse (101)

רָחָב (adj) wide, spacious (20)

רְחוֹב (fs) public square, street (43)

רַחוּם (adj) compassionate (13)

רָחוֹק (adj) distant, remote, far away (84)

רָחַם (Pi) to show love for, have compassion (for), take pity on (47)

רֶ֫חֶם womb (26)

רַחֲמִים compassion, mercy (40)

רָחַץ (Q) to wash (with water), wash (off or away), bathe, bathe oneself (72)

רָחַק (Q) to be(come) far or distant, keep far from; (Hi) remove, put (keep) far away, keep at a distance (59)

רִיב (Q) to strive, contend, quarrel, dispute, conduct a legal case (72)

רִיב dispute, quarrel, lawsuit (62)

רֵיחַ smell, odor, scent (58)

רִיק (Hi) to empty out, pour out (19)

רִיק emptiness, vanity (12)

רֵיק (adj) empty, vain (14)

רֵיקָם empty-handed, without success (16)

רַךְ (adj) tender, frail, weak, soft (16)

רָכַב (Q) to ride, mount and ride; (Hi) cause or make to ride (78)

רֶ֫כֶב chariot, (coll) chariots or chariot riders (120)

רְכוּשׁ goods, property, equipment (28)

רָכַל (Q ptc) to go about as a trader (tradesman), merchant (17)רִמּוֹן
pomegranate, pomegranate tree (33)

רֹ֫מַח spear, lance (15)

רְמִיָּה laziness, slackness, deceit, treachery (15)

רָמַס (Q) to trample (down), tread (potter's clay or grapes), crush to pieces (19)

רָמַשׂ (Q) to crawl, creep, swarm, teem (17)

רֶ֫מֶשׂ creeping thing, animal that creeps upon the earth (17)

רִנָּה shout of joy or lament (33)

רָנַן (Q) to call or cry aloud, shout with joy; (Pi) cry out (with joy), exult (53)

רַע (adj) bad, evil, wicked, worthless; also spelled רָע (312)

רֹ֫עַ corruption, evil (19)

רֵעַ friend, companion, neighbor (188)

רָעֵב (adj) hungry (20)

רָעֵב (Q) to be hungry, suffer famine (13)

רָעָב famine, hunger (101)

רָעָה evil, wickedness, calamity, disaster (354)

רָעָה (Q) to pasture, tend (flocks), graze, shepherd, feed (167)

רַעְיָה darling, beloved (10)

רָעַם (Q) to rage, roar (sea), thunder, storm; (Hi) thunder, storm (11)

רַעֲנָן (adj) green, fresh, luxuriant (19)

רָעַע (Q) to be bad, evil or displeasing; (Hi) do evil, do wickedly, do injury, harm, treat badly (98)

רָעַשׁ (Q) to quake, shake (29)

רַ֫עַשׁ earthquake, clatter, commotion (17)

רָפָא (Q) to heal; (Ni) be healed, become whole; (Pi) heal, make healthy (69)

רָפָה (Q) to sink, drop, relax, grow slack; (Hi) abandon, forsake, desert, leave (someone) alone (46)

רָצָה (Q) to be pleased with, favorable toward, well disposed toward, accept (with pleasure), become friends with (48)

רָצוֹן pleasure, acceptance, favor (56)

רָצַח (Q) to kill, murder, slay (47)

רָצַץ (Q) to crush, oppress, mistreat (19)

רַק only, still, but, however (109)

רָקִיעַ expanse, firmament (17)

רִקְמָה (something) embroidered, woven garment (12)

רָקַע (Q) to stamp (down or out), trample, spread out; (Pi) beat out, hammer out (11)

רָשַׁע (Hi) to condemn, declare or pronounce guilty (35)

רֶ֫שַׁע evil, wickedness, offense, injustice, wrong (30)

רָשָׁע (adj) wicked, guilty (264)

רִשְׁעָה wickedness, guilt (15)

רֶ֫שֶׁת net, trap (22)

שׂ

שְׂבָכָה network, lattice, grid (17)

שָׂבַע (Q) to be satisfied, have one's fill (of), eat or drink one's fill; (Hi) satisfy (97)

שָׂבֵעַ (adj) satisfied, full (10)

שָׂגַב (Ni) to be high, exalted, inaccessible; (Pi) make high, make inaccessible, protect (20)

שָׂדֶה (ms) field, pastureland (329)

שֶׂה (ms) sheep, lamb (47)

שׂוּשׂ (Q) to rejoice; also spelled שִׂישׂ (27)

שְׂחוֹק laughter, laughingstock, mockery (14)

שָׂחַק (Q) to laugh, play; (Pi) play, entertain, dance, amuse (37)

שָׂטָן adversary, accuser, Satan (26)

שֵׂיבָה gray hair, old age (19)

שִׂיחַ (Q) to consider, meditate, complain, lament, praise (20)

שִׂיחַ complaint, lament (14)

שִׂים (Q) to set (up), put, place, set in place, establish; also spelled שׂוּם (588)

שָׂכִיר (adj) hired worker; (n) day laborer (18)

שֶׂכֶל insight, understanding, success; also spelled שֵׂכֶל (16)

שָׂכַל (Hi) to understand, comprehend, have insight, make wise, have success (60)

שָׂכַר (Q) to hire (for wages) (20)

שָׂכָר wages, payment, reward (28)

שַׂלְמָה garment, clothing (16)

שְׂמֹאל left, left side, north; also spelled שְׂמֹאול (54)

שָׂמַח (Q) to rejoice, be joyful, glad; (Pi) cause to rejoice, gladden, make someone happy (156)

שָׂמֵחַ (adj) joyful, glad, happy (21)

שִׂמְחָה joy, gladness (94)

שִׂמְלָה garment, clothing (31)

שָׂנֵא (Q) to hate; (Pi ptc) enemy (148)

שִׂנְאָה hatred, enmity, malice (17)

שָׂעִיר male goat (52)

שֵׂעָר hair, hairiness (28)

שְׂעֹרָה barley; (fp) שְׂעֹרִים (34)

שָׂפָה lip, language, edge, shore (178)

שַׂק sack, sackcloth (48)

שַׂר ruler, prince (421)

שָׂרִיד survivor (29)

שָׂרַף (Q) to burn (completely), destroy; (Ni) be burned (117)

שְׂרֵפָה burning, fire (13)

שָׂשׂוֹן joy, exultation (22)

שׁ

שֶׁ (prefixed rel pron) who, which, that (143)

שָׁאַב (Q) to draw water (19)

שָׁאַג (Q) to roar (21)

שְׁאוֹל (cs) underworld, Sheol (65)

שָׁאוֹן noise, uproar, tumult (17)

שָׁאַל (Q) to ask (of), inquire (of), request, demand (176)

שְׁאֵלָה request, petition (13)

שַׁאֲנָן (adj) at ease, secure, untroubled; (fp) שַׁאֲנַנּוֹת (10)

שָׁאַף (Q) to gasp, pant (for or after), long for (14)

שָׁאַר (Ni) to remain, be left over, survive; (Hi) leave (someone or something) remaining (133)

שְׁאָר remnant, remainder (26)

שְׁאֵר flesh, meat, food, blood relative (16)

שְׁאֵרִית remnant, remainder (66)

שָׁבָה (Q) to take captive, deport (47)

שָׁבוּעַ week, (period of) seven; (mp) שָׁבֻעִים and שָׁבֻעוֹת (20)

שְׁבוּעָה oath; also spelled שְׁבֻעָה (30)

שְׁבוּת captivity, exile, imprisonment (29)

שֵׁ֫בֶט rod, staff, scepter, tribe (190); שִׁבְטֵי יִשְׂרָאֵל "the tribes of Israel"

שְׁבִי captivity, captives (48)

שְׁבִיעִי (adj) seventh; (fs) שְׁבִיעִית (98)

שְׁבִית captivity (14)

שִׁבֹּ֫לֶת ear of grain; (fp) שִׁבֳּלִים (16)

שָׁבַע (Ni) to swear (take) an oath; (Hi) cause to take an oath, plead with someone (186)

שֶׁ֫בַע (ms) seven; (fs) שִׁבְעָה; (mp) שִׁבְעִים seventy (490)

שָׁבַר (Q) to break (up), break in pieces, smash, shatter; (Ni) be smashed, broken, shattered or destroyed; (Pi) shatter, smash, break (148)

שָׁבַר (Q) to buy grain (for food) (21)

שֶׁ֫בֶר break, fracture, collapse (44)

שָׁבַת (Q) to stop, cease, rest; (Hi) put an end to, remove, put away (71)

שַׁבָּת (cs) Sabbath, day or period of rest; (cp) שַׁבָּתוֹת (111)

שַׁבָּתוֹן day of rest, Sabbath, feast (11)

שְׁגָגָה error, accident (19)

שָׁגָה (Q) to stray (of sheep), go astray (morally), err, do or go wrong (unintentionally), stagger, reel (21)

שַׁד breast; (md) שָׁדַיִם (21)

שֹׁד violence, destruction (25)

שָׁדַד (Q) to devastate, ruin, deal violently with, violently destroy; (Pu) be devastated (59)

שַׁדַּי (divine title) Almighty, Shaddai (48); אֵל־שַׁדַּי "God Almighty" (of uncertain etymology)

שֹׁהַם precious stone, carnelian (11)

שָׁוְא worthlessness, vanity, emptiness (54)

שׁוֹאָה trouble, ruin, storm (12)

שׁוּב (Q) to turn back, turn, return; (Hi) cause to return, bring back, restore; (Polel) bring back, restore (1,075)

שָׁוָה (Q) to be(come) like or similar to, be the equal of, resemble; (Pi) make like, make level (16)

שׁוּט (Q) to roam (around), go (rove) about, row (across water); (Polel) roam about (around) (13)

שׁוֹטֵר officer, official (25)

שׁוּל hem, skirt (of robe) (11)

שָׁוַע (Pi) to cry or call for help (21)

שַׁוְעָה cry for help (11)

שׁוֹעֵר gatekeeper (37)

שׁוֹפָר trumpet, ram's horn; (mp) שׁוֹפָרוֹת (72)

שׁוֹק (fs) thigh, leg (19)

שׁוֹר ox, bull, cow (79)

שׁוּר (Q) to behold, regard (15)

שׁוּשַׁן lily, lotus flower; also spelled שׁוֹשָׁן (17)

שָׁזַר (Hoph ptc) twisted; always spelled מָשְׁזָר (21)

שֹׁחַד bribe, gift (23)

שָׁחַח (Q) to cower, crouch, bow down (18)

שָׁחַט (Q) to slaughter (animals for sacrifice) (81)

שְׁחִין boil, blister, skin ulcer (13)

שַׁחַק layer of dust, cloud of dust, cloud (21)

שָׁחַר (Pi) to seek eagerly for, look diligently for, be intent on (12)

שַׁחַר dawn, daybreak (23)

שָׁחַת (Pi, Hi) to ruin, destroy, spoil, annihilate (152)

שַׁחַת pit, grave (23)

שִׁטָּה acacia tree; (fp) שִׁטִּים (28)

שָׁטַף (Q) to flood (over), overflow, rinse, wash (away) (31)

שִׁיר (Q) to sing (of); (Q and Polel ptc) singer (88)

שִׁיר song (78)

שִׁירָה song (13)

שִׁית (Q) to set, put, place, set one's mind to (86)

שָׁכַב (Q) to lie down, have sexual intercourse (with) (213)

שִׁכּוֹר (adj) drunk; (n) drunkard (13)

שָׁכַל (Q) to become childless; (Pi) make someone childless, deprive of children, cause a miscarriage (24)

שָׁכַח (Q) to forget; (Ni) be forgotten (102)

שָׁכַם (Hi) to get up early, rise early, do (something) early (65)

שְׁכֶם shoulder; (with 3ms suff) שִׁכְמוֹ (22)

שָׁכַן (Q) to settle (down), abide, reside, dwell, inhabit; (Pi) abide, dwell (130)

שָׁכֵן neighbor, resident (19)

שָׁכַר (Q) to be(come) drunk; (Pi, Hi) make (someone) drunk (18)

שֵׁכָר intoxicating drink, beer (23)

שֶׁלֶג snow (20)

שָׁלוֹם peace, welfare, wholeness (237)

שָׁלַח (Q) to send, stretch out; (Pi) send, stretch out, send away, expel; (Pu) be sent away (off) (847)

שֻׁלְחָן table; (mp) שֻׁלְחָנוֹת (71)

שָׁלִישׁ officer, third man in a chariot (17)

שְׁלִישִׁי (adj) third; (fs) שְׁלִשִׁית and שְׁלִישִׁיָּה (108)

שָׁלַךְ (Hi) to send, throw, cast; (Hoph) be thrown, cast (125)

שָׁלָל plunder, spoil (74)

שָׁלַל (Q) to plunder, spoil, capture, rob (14)

שָׁלֵם (Q) to be complete, finished; (Pi) complete, finish, make whole, restore, reward; (Hi) bring to completion, consummate (116)

שָׁלֵם (adj) whole, complete, safe (28)

שֶׁלֶם peace offering (87)

שָׁלַף (Q) to draw out (sword), pull out, take out (25)

שָׁלֹשׁ (ms) three; (fs) שְׁלֹשָׁה; (mp) שְׁלֹשִׁים thirty (606)

שִׁלְשׁוֹם day before yesterday, previously (25); תְּמוֹל שִׁלְשֹׁם "yesterday and the day before"

שָׁם there, then, at that time (835)

שֵׁם name, reputation (864)

שָׁמַד (Ni) to be exterminated, destroyed, or annihilated; (Hi) exterminate, annihilate (90)

שַׁמָּה desolation, horror (39)

שְׁמוּעָה message, report, news (27)

שָׁמַט (Q) to let loose, let fall, let drop, release, abandon, leave fallow (10)

שָׁמַ֫יִם heaven, sky (421)

שְׁמִינִי (adj) eighth; (fs) שְׁמִינִית (31)

שָׁמֵם (Q) to be deserted, uninhabited; (Ni) be made uninhabited, desolate, deserted; (Hi) make deserted or desolated (92)

שְׁמָמָה desolation, waste, ruin (56)

שָׁמֵן (adj) fat, rich (10)

שֶׁ֫מֶן oil, fat (193)

שְׁמֹנֶה eight; (fs) שְׁמֹנָה; (mp) שְׁמֹנִים eighty (147)

שָׁמַע (Q) to hear, listen to, understand, obey; (Ni) be heard; (Hi) proclaim (1,165)

שֵׁ֫מַע report, news, rumor (17)

שָׁמַר (Q) to watch (over), guard, keep, observe, preserve, protect, take care of; (Ni) to be kept, protected, on one's guard (469)

שֶׁ֫מֶשׁ (cs) sun (134)

שֵׁן (cs) tooth, ivory (55)

שָׁנָה year; (fp) שָׁנִים (878)

שָׁנָה (Q) to change; (Pi) change, alter, pervert (15)

שֵׁנָה sleep (23)

שֵׁנִי (adj) second; (fs) שֵׁנִית (156)

שָׁנִי scarlet, crimson (42)

שְׁנַ֫יִם (md) two; (fd) שְׁתַּ֫יִם (769)

שָׁסָה (Q) to plunder, spoil (11)

שָׁעָה (Q) to gaze at, look at, look (regard) with favor, be concerned about (13)

שָׁעַן (Ni) to lean (on or against), support oneself on, depend on (22)

שַׁ֫עַר gate (373)

שִׁפְחָה female slave or servant, maidservant (63)

שָׁפַט (Q) to judge, make a judgment, decide (between), settle (a dispute or controversy); (Ni) go to court, plead, dispute (204)

שֶׁ֫פֶט act of judgment, punishment (16)

שְׁפִי barren height; (mp) שְׁפָיִים and שְׁפָיִם (10)

שָׁפַךְ (Q) to pour (out), spill, shed (blood) (117)

שָׁפֵל (Q) to be(come) low, humble, humiliated; (Hi) bring down, overthrow, humiliate (30)

שָׁפָל (adj) low, lowly, humble, deep (17)

שְׁפֵלָה foothills, Shephelah (20)

שָׁקַד (Q) to (keep) watch, be wakeful, vigilant, concerned about, watch over (12)

שָׁקָה (Hi) to give drink (to), irrigate (62)

שִׁקּוּץ abomination, detestable thing (28)

שָׁקַט (Q) to be quiet, peaceful, at peace, at rest; (Hi) give (keep) peace (42)

שָׁקַל (Q) to weigh (out) (23)

שֶׁ֫קֶל shekel, measurement of weight (88)

שָׁקַף (Ni) to look down on (from above); (Hi) look down from above (22)

שֶׁ֫קֶץ detestable thing, abomination (11)

שֶׁ֫קֶר lie, deception, falsehood (113)

שָׁרַץ (Q) to swarm, teem (with), be innumerable (14)

שֶׁ֫רֶץ swarming things (15)

שָׁרַק (Q) to hiss, whistle (12)

שְׁרִרוּת stubbornness, hardness (10)

שֹׁ֫רֶשׁ root; (mp with 3ms suff) שָׁרָשָׁיו (33)

שָׁרַת (Pi) to minister, serve (98)

שֵׁשׁ six; (fs) שִׁשָּׁה; (fs cstr) שֵׁ֫שֶׁת; (mp) שִׁשִּׁים sixty (274)

שֵׁשׁ linen (39)

שִׁשִּׁי (adj) sixth; (fs) שִׁשִּׁית (28)

שָׁתָה (Q) to drink (217)

שָׁתַל (Q) to plant, transplant (10)

ת

תָּא chamber, guardroom (17)

תַּאֲוָה desire, longing (26)

תְּאֵנָה fig tree, fig; (fp) תְּאֵנִים (39)

תֹּ֫אַר form, shape, appearance (15)

תֵּבָה ark, basket, box (28)

תְּבוּאָה produce, harvest (43)

תְּבוּנָה understanding, skill (42)

תֵּבֵל (fs) world (36)

תֶּ֫בֶן straw, chaff (17)

תַּבְנִית pattern, form (20)

תֹּ֫הוּ emptiness, wasteland, formlessness (20)

תְּהוֹם (cs) primeval ocean, deep, depth (36)

תְּהִלָּה praise, song of praise (58)

תַּהְפּוּכָה perversity, perverse thing (10)

תּוֹדָה thanksgiving, song of thanksgiving, thank offering (32)

תּוֹכַ֫חַת rebuke, correction (24)

תּוֹלֵדוֹת (fp) generations, descendants; (fp cstr) תּוֹלְדֹת and תֹּלְדוֹת (39)

תּוֹלַ֫עַת worm (39)

תּוֹעֵבָה abomination, abhorrence, offensive thing (118)

תּוֹצָאוֹת end, limit, outermost area (25)

תּוּר (Q) to spy out, reconnoiter, explore, investigate (24)

תּוֹר (fs) turtledove; (fp) תֹּרִים (14)

תּוֹרָה law, instruction, teaching (223)

תּוֹשָׁב resident alien, stranger, sojourner (14)

תּוּשִׁיָּה wisdom, success (12)

תַּזְנוּת prostitution, fornication (22)

תְּחִלָּה beginning (23)

תְּחִנָּה plea, petition (for favor) (25)

תַּחֲנוּן plea for mercy, supplication (for favor) (18)

תַּ֫חַשׁ porpoise, dolphin, leather (14)

תַּ֫חַת (prep) under, below, instead of (510)

תַּחְתּוֹן (adj) lower, lowest (13)

תַּחְתִּית (fs adj) lower; (fp) תַּחְתִּיּוֹת (19)

תִּיכוֹן (adj) middle, center (11)

תֵּימָן (fs) south; (with directional ה) תֵּימָ֫נָה (24)

תִּירוֹשׁ new wine (38)

תְּכֵ֫לֶת blue or purple material (49)

תָּכַן (Q) to examine, consider, weigh; (Ni) be examined (18)

תָּלָה (Q) to hang (up) (29)

תָּם (adj) blameless, complete, perfect; (mp) תַּמִּים (15)

תֹּם integrity, innocence, perfection; (with 3ms suff) תֻּמּוֹ (23)

תְּמוֹל yesterday, previously (23); תְּמוֹל שִׁלְשׁוֹם "yesterday and the day before"

תְּמוּנָה form, likeness, image (10)

תָּמִיד continually (104)

תָּמִים (adj) blameless, perfect, honest, devout (91)

תָּמַךְ (Q) to grasp, take hold of, hold, support (21)

תָּמַם (Q) to be(come) complete or finished, come to an end, cease, be consumed, burned out (64)

תִּמֹרָה palm tree ornament; (fp) תִּמֹרִים and תִּמֹרוֹת (20)

תַּן (cs) jackal; (cp) תַּנִּים (15)

תְּנוּפָה wave offering, consecrated gift (30)

תַּנּוּר (cs) oven, firepot, furnace (15)

תַּנִּין serpent, dragon, monster (15)

תָּעַב (Pi) to abhor, loathe, commit an abomination (22)

תָּעָה (Q) to err, wander (about), stagger, go astray (animal); (Hi) lead astray, cause to err (51)

תַּ֫עַר razor, knife, sheath (13)

תֹּף tambourine, hand drum; (mp) תֻּפִּים (17)

תִּפְאֶ֫רֶת beauty, glory, splendor (49)

תְּפִלָּה prayer (77)

תָּפַשׂ (Q) to take hold of, seize, capture, grasp; (Ni) be seized, caught, captured, conquered (65)

תִּקְוָה hope, expectation (32)

תָּקַע (Q) to drive or thrust (weapon into a person), pitch (tent), blow (trumpet), clap one's hands (70)

תְּרוּמָה offering, contribution, tribute (76)

תְּרוּעָה shout, alarm, signal (36)

תְּרָפִים images, statues, idols (15)

תְּשׁוּעָה salvation, deliverance, victory (34)

תְּשִׁיעִי (adj) ninth; (fs) תְּשִׁיעִית (18)

תֵּ֫שַׁע nine; (fs) תִּשְׁעָה; (mp) תִּשְׁעִים ninety (78)